Guidebook for Social Work Literature Reviews and Research Questions

GUIDEBOOK FOR SOCIAL WORK LITERATURE REVIEWS AND RESEARCH QUESTIONS

Rebecca L. Mauldin and Matthew DeCarlo

Jandel Crutchfield and Brooke Troutman

Mavs Open Press
Arlington

ISBN 13: 978-0-98988-789-2

4750 Venture Drive, Suite 400
Ann Arbor, MI 48108
800-562-2147
www.xanedu.com

CONTENTS

About the Publisher   vii

About This Project   ix

Acknowledgments   xi

Chapter One: Beginning a research project

1.1 Getting started   2

1.2 Sources of information   10

1.3 Finding literature   22

Chapter Two: Reading and evaluating literature

2.1 Reading an empirical journal article   33

2.2 Evaluating sources   42

2.3 Refining your question   49

Chapter Three: Conducting a literature review

3.1 What is a literature review?   54

3.2 Synthesizing literature   59

3.3 Writing the literature review   68

Chapter 4: Creating and refining a research question

4.1 Empirical versus ethical questions   84

4.2 Writing a good research question   87

4.3 Quantitative research questions   91

4.4 Qualitative research questions   97

4.5 Feasibility and importance   101

4.6 Matching question and design   106

Appendices

Appendix A: Questions for Critiquing Quantitative Research Articles   110

Appendix B: Questions for Critiquing Qualitative Research Articles   113

Glossary   115

Bibliography   118

Derivative Notes   121

ABOUT THE PUBLISHER

About Mavs Open Press

Creation of this resource was supported by Mavs Open Press, operated by the University of Texas at Arlington Libraries (UTA Libraries). Mavs Open Press offers no-cost services for UTA faculty, staff, and students who wish to openly publish their scholarship. The Libraries' program provides human and technological resources that empower our communities to publish new open access journals, to convert traditional print journals to open access publications, and to create or adapt open educational resources (OER). Resources published by Mavs Open Press are openly licensed using Creative Commons licenses and are offered in various e-book formats free of charge. Optional print copies may be available through the UTA Bookstore or can be purchased through print-on-demand services, such as Lulu.com.

About OER

OER are free teaching and learning materials that are licensed to allow for revision and reuse. They can be fully self-contained textbooks, videos, quizzes, learning modules, and more. OER are distinct from public resources in that they permit others to use, copy, distribute, modify, or reuse the content. The legal permission to modify and customize OER to meet the specific learning objectives of a particular course make them a useful pedagogical tool.

About Pressbooks

Pressbooks is a web-based authoring tool based on WordPress, and it is the primary tool that Mavs Open Press (in addition to many other open textbook publishers) uses to create and adapt open textbooks. In May 2018, Pressbooks announced their *Accessibility Policy*, which outlines their efforts and commitment to making their software accessible. Please note that Pressbooks no longer supports use on Internet Explorer as there are important features in Pressbooks that Internet Explorer doesn't support.

The following browsers are best to use for Pressbooks:

- Firefox
- Chrome
- Safari
- Edge

Contact Us

Information about open education at UTA is available online. If you are an instructor who is using this OER for a course, please let us know by filling out our OER Adoption Form. Contact us at oer@uta.edu for other inquires related to UTA Libraries publishing services.

ABOUT THIS PROJECT

Overview

Writing a literature review can be a daunting task for students. Many schools and universities provide writing resources, but it can be time consuming and overwhelming to locate and consume the materials available online. This short guidebook provides information about selecting a research topic and research questions, searching for literature, reading and understanding scholarly writing, and writing a literature review to synthesize what is known and what remains to be learned about a social problem. For students who appreciate the availability of resources on the internet, it also provides links to additional materials. It is our hope that this guide will be an invaluable resource for students completing an assignment, working as research assistants, or conducting their own research. It can be used with its companion textbook, *Foundations of Social Work Research* by Rebecca L. Mauldin and Matthew DeCarlo, or as a stand alone guide.

Creation Process

In the summer of 2019, Dr. Rebecca L. Mauldin coordinated a project to adopt an open textbook for the School of Social Work's Research Methods courses across the BSW and MSW programs. In that project, she used *Scientific Inquiry in Social Work* by Matthew DeCarlo as a source text. That book included much of the material in this guidebook. This guide was developed from it to provide a comprehensive, yet focused and accessible introduction to conducting literature reviews for social work research. It is intended to be used by a wide range of students from undergraduate and graduates to help understand the rationale, approach, and methods for conducting literature reviews. We anticipate it being used as a textbook in Research Methods courses, but also as an independent guide for students writing research proposals or theses or for first year doctoral students with limited experience writing literature reviews.

About the Author

Rebecca L. Mauldin is an assistant professor at the University of Texas at Arlington's School of Social Work. Dr. Mauldin's research interests include social networks, social support, gerontology, and generosity. Her research focuses on the role of social relationships in the health and well-being of older adults. She examines the resources and benefits associated with relationships among residents of long-term care facilities, older immigrants, and older adults aging in place. Collaborative in nature, Dr. Mauldin enjoys community practice, program development, and coalition building. She thrives in teaching environments and brings forth others' strengths in her practice, scholarship, and teaching.

ACKNOWLEDGMENTS

UTA CARES Grant Program

Creation of this OER was funded by the UTA CARES Grant Program, which is sponsored by UTA Libraries. Under the auspices of UTA's Coalition for Alternative Resources in Education for Students (CARES), the grant program supports educators interested in practicing open education through the adoption of OER and, when no suitable open resource is available, through the creation of new OER or the adoption of library-licensed or other free content. Additionally, the program promotes innovation in teaching and learning through the exploration of open educational practices, such as collaborating with students to produce educational content of value to a wider community. Information about the grant program and funded projects is available online.

Author's Note

This guidebook to writing literature reviews would not be possible without the source material. Dr. DeCarlo's textbook is a comprehensive introduction to social work research methods. I am grateful to him for his generosity and support. I would like to thank Michelle Reed of the UTA Libraries for sharing their extensive knowledge and their guidance in compiling this guide. Also from the UTA Libraries, Brooke Troutman provided guidance and contributed material. Amanda Steed worked many hours to assist in this book's creation and offered incisive insights to make this guide as useful to students as possible. My appreciation also goes out to Teresa McIntyre, Diane Mitschke, and Regina Praetorius, three faculty members at the UTA School of Social Work, who reviewed the original source material for this guidebook and offered their suggestions for this guide. Finally, I thank Jandel Crutchfield, also of UTA's School of Social Work, for contributing material to the guidebook.

Project Lead

Rebecca L. Mauldin – Assistant Professor, University of Texas at Arlington

Contributors

Jandel Crutchfield – Assistant Professor, University of Texas at Arlington

Matthew DeCarlo – Assistant Professor, Radford University

Brooke Troutman – Assistant Librarian, University of Texas at Arlington

About the Cover

Brittany Griffiths, UTA Libraries' Publishing Specialist, designed the cover for this OER. The images used were taken by Ruben Espiricueta and were used with his permission.

CHAPTER ONE: BEGINNING A RESEARCH PROJECT

For many students, designing a research project is an opportunity to explore a social problem that interests them. There is wide variety of social work research questions that can be addressed with research projects. At the beginning a question looms large: what research topic should you choose?

Chapter outline

- 1.1 Getting started
- 1.2 Sources of information
- 1.3 Finding literature

Content advisory

This chapter discusses or mentions the following topics: racism and hate groups, racial disparities in schools, police violence, substance abuse, and mental health.

1.1 GETTING STARTED

Learning Objectives
• Find a topic to investigate • Create a working question

Choosing a social work research topic

According to the Action Network for Social Work Education and Research (ANSWER), social work research is conducted to benefit "consumers, practitioners, policymakers, educators, and the general public through the examination of societal issues" (Action Network for Social Work Education and Research, ANSWER, n.d., para. 2). Common social issues that are studied include "health care, substance abuse, community violence, family issues, child welfare, aging, well-being and resiliency, and the strengths and needs of underserved populations" (ANSWER, n.d., para. 2). This list is certainly not exhaustive. Social workers may study any area that impacts their practice. However, the unifying feature of social work research is its focus on promoting the well-being of target populations.

But as social work students, you may not be practicing social work yet. How do you identify valuable research topics then? Part of the joy in being a social work student is figuring out what areas of social work are appealing to you. Perhaps there are certain theories that speak to you, based on your values or experiences. Perhaps there are social issues you wish to change. Perhaps there are certain groups of people you want to help. Perhaps there are clinical interventions that interest you. Any one of these is a good place to start. At the beginning of a research project, your main focus should be finding a social work topic that is interesting enough to spend a semester reading and writing about it.

A good topic selection plan begins with a general orientation into the subject you are interested in pursuing in more depth. Here are some suggestions when choosing a topic area:

- Pick an interest, experience, or an area where you know there is a need for more research.
- It may be easier to start with "what" and "why" questions and expand on those. For example, what are the best methods of treating severe depression? Or why are people receiving SNAP more likely to be obese?
- If you already have practice experience in social work through employment, an

internship, or volunteer work, think about practice issues you noticed in the placement.

- Ask a professor, preferably one active in research, about possible topics.
- Read departmental information on research interests of the faculty. Faculty research interests vary widely, and it might surprise you what they've published on in the past. Most departmental websites post the curriculum vitae, or CV, of faculty which lists their publications, credentials, and interests.
- Read a research paper that interests you. The paper's literature review or background section will provide insight into the research question the author was seeking to address with their study. Is the research incomplete, imprecise, biased, or inconsistent? As you're reading the paper, look for what's missing. These may be "gaps in the literature" that you might explore in your own study. The conclusion or discussion section at the end may also offer some questions for future exploration. A recent blog posting in *Science* (Pain, 2016) provides several tips from researchers and graduate students on how to effectively read these papers.
- Think about papers you enjoyed researching and writing in other classes. Research is a unique class and will use the tools of social science for you to think more in depth about a topic. It will bring a new perspective that will deepen your knowledge of the topic.
- Identify and browse journals related to your research interests. Faculty and librarians can help you identify relevant journals in your field and specific areas of interest.

Spotlight on UTA: Dr. Jandel Crutchfield

Before Dr. Jandel Crutchfield of the University of Texas at Arlington's School of Social Work ever became a school social worker or a social work professor, she was "just" a student in public schools in southern Louisiana. While she had a very strong support system through her family and community, she remembers interacting with students around her who clearly did not have the same set of life circumstances that she did. And she saw, too, that often those circumstances interfered with their performance at school. She served as a mentor during her middle and high school years to try to stand in the gap for some of these students who were facing personal and/or academic challenges, and so, it came naturally that she would want to become a school social worker as a long-term career. Whether it was her years of schooling as a child or as a professional working in K-12 public schools, she experienced enough to come up with at least 20 different research topics related to schools. Not only was school such a pivotal part of life for children and families, but there was so much happening in schools that influenced long term outcomes like employment, safety, freedom, and success!

Dr. Jandel Crutchfield of University of Texas at Arlington's School of Social Work

Of all these 20+ potential topics, she really wanted to know how social workers could help improve the lives of children and families in schools. When she began exploring research articles, she found it interesting to see there existed lots of ideas and models of how school social workers could assist students with academic, social, behavioral, and psychological health in schools. But based on her experience, she saw several gaps in these models and ideas. In the literature about school social work, she didn't find much information about school social workers working with minority (black and brown) students. She remembered in her own personal and professional experiences that minority students make up a large percentage of the public school students and that they were experiencing very consequential racial disparities in academic success and school discipline. So, she launched out to explore what became her first research topic: exactly what school social workers are doing to address these disparities. From this topic, another research area blossomed, as she discovered that many school social workers reported a desire to address racial disparities but lack the cultural competence training to advocate effectively for anti-racist interventions. And so, her research quest also involves seeking out understanding of cultural competence needs in school social work practice. She's very thankful that her own personal and professional experiences served her well in finding research topics. She found two pathways to explore minority student experience: school social work interventions for minority students and cultural competence among school social workers (for more information, refer to Crutchfield & Webb, 2018; Crutchfield, Crutchfield, & Buford, 2018; Ortega-Williams, Crutchfield, & Hall (in press); and Tan, Teasley, Crutchfield & Canfield, 2017).

How do you feel about your topic?

Perhaps you have started with a specific population in mind—for example, youth who identify as LGBTQ or visitors to a local health clinic. In other cases, you may start with a social problem, such as gang violence, or social policy or program, such as zero-tolerance policies in schools. Alternately, maybe there are interventions like dialectical behavioral therapy or applied behavior analysis about which you would like to learn more. Your motivation for choosing a topic does not have to be objective. Because social work is a values-based profession, social work researchers often find themselves motivated to conduct research that furthers social justice or fights oppression. Just because you think a policy is wrong or a group is being marginalized, for example, does not mean that your research will be biased. However, it does mean you need to understand how you feel, why you feel that way, and what would cause you to feel differently about your topic.

Start by asking yourself how you feel about your topic. Be totally honest, and ask yourself whether you believe your perspective is the only valid one. Perhaps yours isn't the only perspective, but do you believe it is the wisest one? The most practical one? How do you feel about other perspectives on this topic? If you feel so strongly that certain findings would upset you or that either you would design a project to get only the answer you believe to be the best one or you might feel compelled to cover up findings that you don't like, then you need to choose a different topic. For example, a researcher may want to find out whether there is any relationship between intelligence and political party affiliation—certain that members of her party are without a doubt the most intelligent. Her strong opinion would not be a problem by itself. However, if she feels rage when considering the possibility that the opposing party's members are more intelligent than those of her party, the topic is probably too near and dear for her to use it to conduct unbiased research.

Of course, just because you feel strongly about a topic does not mean that you should not study it. Sometimes the best topics to research are those about which you do feel strongly. What better way to stay motivated than to study something that you care about? You must be able to accept that people will have a different perspective than you do, and try to represent their viewpoints fairly in your research. If you feel prepared to accept all findings, even those that may be unflattering to or distinct from your personal perspective, then perhaps you should intentionally study a topic about which you have strong feelings.

Kathleen Blee (1991, 2002) has taken this route in her research. Blee studies hate movement participants, people whose racist ideologies she studies but does not share. You can read her accounts of this research in two of her most well-known publications, *Inside Organized Racism* and *Women of the Klan*. Blee's research is successful because she was willing to report her findings and observations honestly, even those about which she may have strong feelings. Unlike Blee, if you think about it and conclude that you cannot accept or share with others findings with which you disagree, then you should study a different topic. Knowing your own hot-button issues is an important part of self-knowledge and reflection in social work.

Social workers often use personal experience as a starting point for what topics are interesting to cover. As we've discussed here, personal experience can be a powerful motivator to study a topic in detail. However, social work researchers should be mindful of their own mental health during the research process. A social worker who has experienced a mental health crisis or traumatic event should approach researching related topics cautiously. There is no need to retraumatize yourself or jeopardize your mental health for a research paper. For example, a student who has just experienced domestic violence may want to know about Eye Movement Desensitization and Reprocessing (EMDR) therapy. While the student might gain some knowledge about potential treatments for domestic violence, she will likely have to read through many stories and reports about domestic violence. Unless the student's trauma has been processed in therapy, conducting a research project on this topic may negatively impact the student's mental health. Nevertheless, she will acquire skills in research methods that will help her understand the EMDR literature and whether to begin treatment in that modality.

Whether you feel strongly about your topic or not, you will also want to consider what you already known about it. There are many ways we know what we know. Perhaps your mother told you something is so. Perhaps it came to you in a dream. Perhaps you took a class last semester and learned something about your topic there. Or you may have read something about your topic in your local newspaper or in *People* magazine. We discussed the strengths and weaknesses associated with some of these different sources of knowledge in Chapter 1, and we'll talk about other sources of knowledge, such as prior research in the next few sections. For now, take some time to think about what you know about your topic from all possible sources. Thinking about what you already know will help you identify any biases you may have, and it will help as you begin to frame a question about your topic.

What do you want to know?

Once you have a topic, begin to think about it in terms of a question. What do you really want to know about the topic? As a warm-up exercise, try dropping a possible topic idea into one of the blank spaces below. The questions may help bring your subject into sharper focus and provide you with the first important steps towards developing your topic.

1. What does ___ mean? (Definition)
2. What are the various features of ___? (Description)
3. What are the component parts of ___? (Simple analysis)
4. How is ___ made or done? (Process analysis)
5. How should ___ be made or done? (Directional analysis)
6. What is the essential function of ___? (Functional analysis)
7. What are the causes of ___? (Causal analysis)
8. What are the consequences of ___? (Causal analysis)
9. What are the types of ___? (Classification)
10. How is ___ like or unlike ___? (Comparison)
11. What is the present status of ___? (Comparison)
12. What is the significance of ___? (Interpretation)
13. What are the facts about ___? (Reportage)
14. How did ___ happen? (Narration)
15. What kind of person is ___? (Characterization/Profile)
16. What is the value of ___? (Evaluation)
17. What are the essential major points or features of ___? (Summary)
18. What case can be made for or against ___? (Persuasion)
19. What is the relationship between _____ and the outcome of _____? (Explorative)

Take a minute right now and write down a question you want to answer. Even if it doesn't seem perfect, everyone needs a place to start. Make sure your research topic is relevant to social work. You'd be surprised how much of the world that encompasses. It's not just research on mental health treatment or child welfare services. Social workers can study things like the pollution of irrigation systems and entrepreneurship in women, among infinite other topics. The only requirement is your research must inform action to fight social problems faced by target populations.

Your question is only a starting place, as research is an *iterative process*, one that subject to constant revision. As we progress in this textbook, you'll learn how to refine your question and include the necessary components for proper qualitative and quantitative research questions. Your question will also likely change as you engage with the literature on your topic. You will learn new and important concepts that may shift your focus or clarify your original ideas. Trust that a strong question will emerge from this process.

Key Takeaways

- Many researchers choose topics by considering their own personal experiences, knowledge, and interests.
- Researchers should be aware of and forthcoming about any strong feelings they might have about their research topics.
- There are benefits and drawbacks associated with studying a topic about which you already have some prior knowledge or experience. Researchers should be aware of and consider both.
- Writing a question down will help guide your inquiry.

Image Attributions

Transportation/Traffic by Geralt CC-0

Justice by Geralt CC-0

Question by Max Pixel CC-0

1.2 SOURCES OF INFORMATION

Because a literature review is a summary and analysis of the relevant publications on a topic, we first have to understand what is meant by "the literature." In this case, "the literature" is a collection of all of the relevant written sources on a topic.

Disciplines of knowledge

When drawing boundaries around an idea, topic, or subject area, it helps to think about how and where the information for the field is produced. For this, you need to identify the disciplines of knowledge production in a subject area.

Information does not exist in the environment like some kind of raw material. It is produced by individuals working within a particular field of knowledge (or **discipline**) who use specific methods for generating new information. Disciplines consume, produce, and disseminate knowledge. Looking through a university's course catalog gives clues to disciplinary structure. Fields such as political science, biology, history, and mathematics are unique disciplines, as is social work, with its own logic for how and where new knowledge is introduced and made accessible.

You will need to become comfortable with identifying the disciplines that might contribute information to any search. When you do this, you will also learn how to decode the way how people talk about a topic within a discipline. This will be useful to you when you begin a review of the literature in your area of study.

For example, think about the disciplines that might contribute information to a topic such as the role of sports in society. Try to anticipate the type of perspective each discipline might have on the topic. Consider the following types of questions as you examine what different disciplines might contribute:

- What is important about the topic to the people in that discipline?
- What is most likely to be the focus of their study about the topic?
- What perspective would they be likely to have on the topic?

In this example, we identify two disciplines that have something to say about the role of sports in society: the human service professions of nursing and social work. What would each of these disciplines raise as key questions or issues related to that topic? A nursing researcher might study how sports affect individuals' health and well-being, how to assess and treat sports injuries, or the physical conditioning required for athletics. A social work researcher might study how schools privilege or punish student athletes, how athletics impact social relationships and hierarchies, or the differences between boys' and girls' participation in organized sports. In this example, we see that a single topic can be approached from many different perspectives depending on how the disciplinary boundaries are drawn and how the topic is framed. Nevertheless, it is useful for a social worker to be aware of the nursing literature, as they could better appreciate the physical toll that sports take on athletes' bodies and how that may interact with other issues. An interdisciplinary perspective is usually a more comprehensive perspective.

Types of sources of information

"The literature" consists of the published works that document a scholarly conversation on a specific topic within and between disciplines. In "the literature," you will find documents that explain the background of your topic. You will also find controversies and unresolved questions that can inspire your own project. By now in your social work academic career, you've probably heard that you need to get "peer-reviewed journal articles." But what are those exactly? How do they differ from news articles or encyclopedias? That is the focus of this section of the textbook—the different types of literature.

Periodicals

First, let's discuss **periodicals**. Periodicals include magazines, newspapers, trade publications, and journals. While they may appear similar, particularly online, each of these periodicals has unique features designed for a specific purpose. Magazine and newspaper articles are usually written by journalists, are intended to be short and understandable for the average adult, contain color images and advertisements, and are designed as commodities sold to an audience. Magazines may contain primary or secondary literature depending on the article in question. The *New Social Worker* is an excellent magazine for social workers. An article that is a **primary source** would gather information as an event happened, like an interview with a victim of a local fire, or relate original research done by the journalists, like the Guardian newspaper's *The Counted* webpage which tracks how many people were killed by police officers in the United States (The Guardian, n.d.).

Is it okay to use a magazine or newspaper as a source in your research methods class? In most social work research classes, the answer is "probably not." There are some exceptions like the *Guardian* page mentioned above or breaking news about a policy or community, but most of what newspapers and magazines publish is secondary literature. **Secondary sources** interpret, discuss, and summarize primary sources. Often, news articles will summarize a study done in an academic journal. Your job in this course is to *read the original source of the information*, in this case, the academic journal article itself. Journalists are not scientists. If you have seen articles about how chocolate cures cancer or how drinking whiskey can extend your life, you should understand how journalists can exaggerate or misinterpret results. Careful scholars will critically examine the primary source, rather than relying on someone else's summary. Many newspapers and magazines also contain **opinion articles**, which are even less reputable as the author will choose facts to support their viewpoint and exclude facts that contract their viewpoint. Nevertheless, newspaper and magazine articles are excellent places to start your journey into the literature, as they do not require specialized knowledge to understand and may inspire deeper inquiry.

Unlike magazines and newspapers, trade publications may take some specialized knowledge to understand. Trade publications or trade journals are periodicals directed to members of a specific profession. They often have information about industry trends and practical information for people working in the field. Because of this trade publications are somewhat more reputable than newspapers or magazines, as the authors are specialists on their field. *NASW News* is a good example a trade publication in social work, published by the National Association of Social Workers. Its intended audience is social work practitioners who want to know about important practice issues. They report news and trends in a field but not scholarly research. They may also provide product or service reviews, job listings, and advertisements.

So, can you use trade publications in a formal research proposal? Again, in most classes, the answer would be "probably not." A main shortcoming trade publication is the lack of peer review. **Peer review** refers to a formal process in which other esteemed researchers and experts ensure your work meets the standards and expectations of the professional field. While trade publications do contain a staff of editors, the level of review is not as stringent as academic journal articles. On the other hand, if you are doing a study about practitioners, then trade publications may be quite relevant sources for your proposal. Peer review is part of the cycle of publication illustrated below and acts as a gatekeeper, ensuring that only top-quality articles are published. While peer review is far from perfect, the process provides for stricter scrutiny of scientific publications.

In summary, newspapers and other popular press publications are useful for getting general topic ideas. Trade publications are useful for practical application in a profession and may also be a good source of keywords for future searching. Scholarly journals are the conversation of the scholars who are doing research in a specific discipline and publishing their research findings.

Journal Articles

As you've probably heard by now, academic journal articles are considered to be the most reputable sources of information, particularly in research methods courses. Journal articles are written by scholars with the intended audience of other scholars (like you!) interested in the subject matter. The articles are often long and contain extensive references for the arguments made by the author. The journals themselves are often dedicated to a single topic, like violence or child welfare, and include articles that seek to advance the body of knowledge about their chosen topic.

Most journals are peer-reviewed or refereed, which means a panel of volunteer scholars reviews articles to decide if they should be accepted into a specific publication and make recommendations for improving them. Scholarly journals provide articles of interest to experts or researchers in a discipline. An editor or editorial board of respected scholars reviews all articles submitted to a journal. Editors and volunteer reviewers decide if the article provides a noteworthy contribution to the field and should be published. For this reason, journal articles are the main source of information for researchers and for literature reviews. You can tell whether a journal is peer reviewed by going to its website. Usually, under the "About Us" section, the website will list the editorial board or otherwise note its procedures for peer review. If a journal does not provide such information, you may have found a "predatory journal." These journals will publish any article—no matter how bad it is—as long as the author pays them. Not all journals are created equal!

A kind of peer review also occurs after publication. Scientists regularly read articles and use them to inform their research. A **seminal article** is "a classic work of research literature that is more than 5 years old and is marked by its uniqueness and contribution to professional knowledge" (Houser, 2018, p. 112). Basically, it is a really important article. Seminal articles are cited a lot in the literature. You can see how many authors have cited an article using Google Scholar's citation count feature when you search for the article. Generally speaking, articles that have been cited more often are considered more reputable. There is nothing wrong with citing an article with a low citation count, but it is an indication that not many other scholars have found the source to be useful or important.

Journal articles fall into a few different categories. **Empirical articles** report the results of a quantitative or qualitative data analysis conducted by the author. Just because an article includes quantitative or qualitative results does not mean it is an empirical journal article. Since most articles contain a literature review with empirical findings, you need to make sure the findings reported in the study are from the author's own analysis. Fortunately, empirical articles follow a similar structure—introduction, method, results, and discussion sections appear in that order. While the exact headings may differ slightly from publication to publication and other sections like conclusions, implications, or limitations may appear, this general structure applies to nearly all empirical journal articles.

Theoretical articles, by contrast, do not follow a set structure. They follow whatever format the author finds most useful to organize their information. Theoretical articles discuss a theory, conceptual model, or framework for understanding a problem. They may delve into philosophy or values, as well. Theoretical articles help you understand how to think about a topic and may help you make sense of the results of empirical studies. **Practical articles** describe "how things are done" (Wallace & Wray, 2016, p. 20). They are usually shorter than other types of articles and are intended to inform practitioners of a discipline on current issues. They may also provide a reflection on a "hot topic" in the practice domain, a complex client situation, or an issue that may affect the profession as a whole.

No one type of article is better than the other, as each serves a different purpose. Seminal articles relevant to your topic area are important to read because of their influence on the field. Theoretical articles will help you understand the social theory behind your topic. Empirical articles should test those theories quantitatively or create those theories qualitatively, a process we will discuss in greater detail later in this book. Practical articles will help you understand a practitioner's perspective, though these are less useful when writing a literature review as they only present a single person's opinions on a topic.

Other sources of information

As mentioned previously, newspaper and magazine articles are good places to start your search (though they should not be the end of your search!). Another source students go to almost immediately is Wikipedia. Wikipedia is a marvel of human knowledge. It is a digital encyclopedia to which anyone can contribute. The entries for each Wikipedia article are overseen by skilled and specialized editors who volunteer their time and knowledge to making sure their articles are correct and up to date. Wikipedia is an example of a tertiary source. We reviewed primary and secondary sources in the previous section. **Tertiary sources** synthesize or distill primary and secondary sources. Examples of tertiary sources include encyclopedias, directories, dictionaries, and textbooks like this one. Tertiary sources are an excellent place to start (but are not a good place to end your search). A student might consult Wikipedia or the Encyclopedia of Social Work to get a general idea of the topic.

The difference between secondary and tertiary sources is not exact, and as we've discussed, using one or both at the beginning of a project is a good idea. As your study of the topic progresses, you will naturally have to transition away from secondary and tertiary sources and towards primary sources. We've already talked about one particular kind of primary source—the academic journal article. We will spend more time on this primary source than any other in this textbook. However, it is important to understand how other types of sources can be used as well.

Books

Books contain important scholarly information. They are particularly helpful for theoretical, philosophical, and historical inquiry. You can use books to learn definitions, key concepts, and keywords you can use to find additional sources. They will help you understand the scope and foundations of a topic and how it has changed over time. Some books contain chapters that look like academic journal articles. These are called *edited volumes*, and they contain articles that may not have made it into academic journals or seminal articles that are republished in the book. Edited volumes are considered less reputable than journal articles, as they do not have as strong of a peer review process. However, papers in social science journals will often include references to books and edited volumes.

Conference proceedings

Conferences are a great source of information. At conferences such as the Council on Social Work Education's Annual Program Meeting or your state's NASW conference, researchers present papers on their most recent research and obtain feedback from the audience. The papers presented at conferences are sometimes published in a volume called a conference proceeding. Conference proceedings highlight current discussion in a discipline and can lead you to scholars who are interested in specific research areas. A word about conference papers: several factors contribute to making these documents difficult to find. It is not unusual that papers delivered at professional conferences are not published in print or electronic form, although an abstract may be available. In these cases, the full paper may only be available from the author or authors. The most important thing to remember is that if you have any difficulty finding a conference proceeding or paper, ask a librarian for assistance.

Gray literature

Another source of information is the **gray literature**, which is research and information released by non-commercial publishers, such as government agencies, policy organizations, and think-tanks. The main shortcoming of gray literature is the lack of peer review that is found in academic journal articles, though many gray literature sources are of good quality and can be good sources of data to describe a social problem. If you have already taken a policy class, perhaps you've come across the Center on Budget and Policy Priorities. CBPP is a think tank or a group of scholars that conduct research and perform advocacy on social issues. Similarly, students often find the Centers for Disease Control website helpful for understanding the prevalence of social problems like mental illness and child abuse. Think tanks and policy organizations often have a specific viewpoint they support. There are conservative, liberal, and libertarian think tanks, for example. Policy organizations may be funded by private businesses to push a given message to the public.

Government data

Government agencies are generally more objective, though they may be less critical of government programs than other sources might be. Some examples of excellent government sources are the U.S. Census Bureau's American FactFinder and data from the Substance Abuse and Mental Health Services Administration, or SAMHSA.

Dissertations

Dissertations and theses can be rich sources of information and have extensive reference lists to scan for resources. They are considered gray literature because they are not peer reviewed. The accuracy and validity of the paper itself may depend on the school that awarded the doctoral or master's degree to the author. If you come across a dissertation that is relevant, it is a good idea to read the literature review and plumb the sources the author uses in your literature search. However, the data analysis from these sources is considered less reputable as it has not passed through peer review yet. Consider searching for journal articles by the author to see if any of the results passed peer review.

Web pages

The final source of information we must talk about is webpages. Matthew DeCarlo's graduate research focused on substance abuse and drugs, and he was fond of reading Drug War Rant, a blog about drug policy. It provided him with breaking news about drug policy and editorial opinion about the drug war. He wouldn't cite the blog in a research proposal, but it was an excellent source of information that warranted further investigation. Web pages will also help you locate professional organizations and human service agencies that address your problem. Looking at their social media feeds, reports, publications, or "news" sections on an organization's web page can clue you into important topics to study. Because anyone can begin their own web page, they are usually not considered scholarly sources to use in formal writing, but they are still useful when you are first learning about a topic. Additionally, many advocacy web pages will provide references for the facts they site, providing you with the primary source of the information.

Evaluating other sources

As you think about each source, remember:

> All information sources are not created equal. Sources can vary greatly in terms of how carefully
> they are researched, written, edited, and reviewed for accuracy. Common sense will help you
> identify obviously questionable sources, such as tabloids that feature tales of alien abductions, or
> personal websites with glaring typos. Sometimes, however, a source's reliability—or lack of it—is

not so obvious…You will consider criteria such as the type of source, its intended purpose and audience, the author's (or authors') qualifications, the publication's reputation, any indications of bias or hidden agendas, how current the source is, and the overall quality of the writing, thinking, and design. (Writing for Success, 2015, p. 448).

While each of these sources is an important part of how we learn about a topic, your research should focus on finding academic journal articles about your topic. These are the primary sources of the research world. While it may be acceptable and necessary to use other primary sources—like books, government reports, or an investigative article by a newspaper or magazine—academic journal articles are preferred. Finding these journal articles is the topic of the next section.

Key Takeaways

- Social work involves reading research from a variety of disciplines.
- While secondary and tertiary sources are okay to start with, primary sources provide the most accurate and authoritative information about a topic.
- Peer-reviewed journal articles are considered the best source of information for literature reviews, though other sources are often used.
- Peer review is the process by which other scholars evaluate the merits of an article before publication.
- Social work research requires critical evaluation of each source in a literature review

Glossary

- Empirical articles- apply theory to a behavior and reports the results of a quantitative or qualitative data analysis conducted by the author
- Gray literature- research and information released by non-commercial publishers, such as government agencies, policy organizations, and think-tanks
- Peer review- a formal process in which other esteemed researchers and experts ensure your work meets the standards and expectations of the professional field
- Practical articles- describe "how things are done" in practice (Wallace & Wray, 2016, p. 20)
- Primary source- published results of original research studies
- Secondary source- interpret, discuss, summarize original sources
- Seminal articles– classic work noted for its contribution to the field and high citation count
- Tertiary source- synthesize or distill primary and secondary sources, such as Wikipedia
- Theoretical articles – articles that discuss a theory, conceptual model or framework for understanding a problem

1.3 FINDING LITERATURE

One of the drawbacks (or joys, depending on your perspective) of being a researcher in the 21st century is that we can do much of our work without ever leaving the comfort of our recliners. This is certainly true of familiarizing yourself with the literature. Most libraries offer incredible online search options and access to important databases of academic journal articles.

A literature search usually follows these steps:
1. Building search queries
2. Finding the right database
3. Skimming the abstracts of articles
4. Looking at author and journal names
5. Examining references
6. Searching for meta-analyses and systematic reviews

Step 1: Building a search query with keywords

What do you type when you are searching for something on Google? Are you a question-asker? Do you type in full sentences or just a few keywords? What you type into a database or search engine like Google is called a **query**. Well-constructed queries get you to the information you need faster, while unclear queries will force you to sift through dozens of irrelevant articles before you find the ones you want.

The words you use in your search query will determine the results you get. Unfortunately, different studies often use different words to mean the same thing. A study may describe its topic as substance abuse, while another discusses substance misuse. Think of different keywords that are relevant to your topic area and write them down. Often in social work research, there is a bit of jargon to learn in crafting your search queries. If you wanted to learn more about people of low-income who do not have access to a bank account, you may need to learn the jargon term "unbanked," which refers to people without bank accounts, and include "unbanked" in your search query. If you wanted to learn about children who take on parental roles in families, you may need to include "parentification" as part of your search query. As student researchers, you are not expected to know these terms ahead of time. Instead, start with the keywords you already know. Once you read more about your topic, start including new keywords that will return the most relevant search results for you.

Google is a "natural language" search engine, which means it tries to use its knowledge of how people to talk to better understand your query. Google's academic database, Google Scholar, incorporates that same approach. However, other databases that are important for social work research—such as Academic Search Complete, PSYCinfo, and PubMed—will not return useful results if you ask a question or type a sentence or phrase as your search query. Instead, these databases are best used by typing in keywords. Instead of typing "the effects of cocaine addiction on the quality of parenting," you might type in "cocaine AND parenting" or "addiction AND child development." Note: you would not actually use the quotation marks in your search query for these examples.

These operators (AND, OR, NOT) are part of what is called Boolean searching. Boolean searching works like a simple computer program. Your search query is made up of words connected by operators. Searching for "cocaine AND parenting" returns articles that mention *both* cocaine and parenting. There are lots of articles on cocaine and lots of articles on parenting, but fewer articles on both of those topics. In this way, the AND operator reduces the number of results you will get from your search query because both terms must be present. The NOT operator also reduces the number of results you get from your query. For example, perhaps you wanted to exclude issues related to pregnancy. Searching for "cocaine AND parenting NOT pregnancy" would exclude articles that mentioned pregnancy from your results. Conversely, the OR operator would increase the number of results you get from your query. For example, searching for "cocaine OR parenting" would return not only articles that mentioned both words but also those that mentioned only one of your two search terms. This relationship is visualized in Figure 1.1 below.

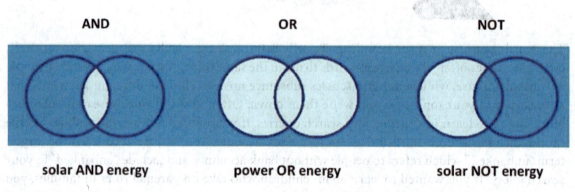

Figure 1.1 Boolean queries

Possibly the most frustrating part about literature searching is looking at the number of search results for your query. How could anyone be expected to look at hundreds of thousands of articles on a topic? Don't worry. You don't have to read all those articles to know enough about your topic area to produce a good research study. A good search query should bring you to at least a few relevant articles to your topic, which is more than enough to get you started. However,

1. Figure 1.1 copied from image "Search operators" by TU Delft Libraries (2017). Shared using a CC-BY 4.0 license .

an excellent search query can narrow down your results to a much smaller number of articles, all of which are specifically focused on your topic area. Here are some tips for reducing the number of articles in your topic area:

1. Use quotation marks to indicate exact phrases, like "mental health" or "substance abuse."
2. Search for your keywords in the ABSTRACT. A lot of your results may be from articles about irrelevant topics simply that mention your search term once. If your topic isn't in the abstract, chances are the article isn't relevant. You can be even more restrictive and search for your keywords in the TITLE. Academic databases provide these options in their advanced search tools.
3. Use multiple keywords in the same query. Simply adding "addiction" onto a search for "substance abuse" will narrow down your results considerably.
4. Use a SUBJECT heading like "substance abuse" to get results from authors who have tagged their articles as addressing the topic of substance abuse. Subject headings are likely to not have all the articles on a topic but are a good place to start.
5. Narrow down the years of your search. Unless you are gathering historical information about a topic, you are unlikely to find articles older than 10-15 years to be useful. They no longer tell you the current knowledge on a topic. All databases have options to narrow your results down by year.
6. Talk to a librarian. They are professional knowledge-gatherers, and there is often a librarian assigned to your department. Their job is to help you find what you need to know.

Step 2: Finding the right database

Four databases you will likely find helpful for finding academic journal articles relevant to social work are: Google Scholar, Academic Search Complete, PsycINFO, and PubMed. Each has distinct advantages and disadvantages.

Because **Google Scholar** is a natural language search engine, you are more likely to get what you want without having to fuss with wording. It can be linked via Library Links to your university login, allowing you to access journal articles with one click on the Google Scholar page. Google Scholar also allows you to save articles in folders and provides a (somewhat correct) APA citation for each article. However, Google Scholar also will automatically display not only journal articles, but books, government and foundation reports, and gray literature. You need to make sure that the source you are using is reputable. Look for the advanced search feature to narrow down your results further.

Academic Search Complete is available through your school's library, under the page titled databases. It is similar to Google Scholar in its breadth, as it contains a number of smaller databases from a variety of social science disciplines (including Social Work Abstracts). You have to use Boolean searching techniques, and there are a number of advanced search features to further narrow down your results.

PsycINFO and **PubMed** focus on specific disciplines. PsycINFO indexes articles on psychology, and PubMed indexes articles related to medical science. Because these databases are more narrowly targeted, you are more likely to get the specific psychological or medical knowledge you desire. If you were to use a more general search engine like Google Scholar, you may get more irrelevant results. Finally, it is worth mentioning that many university libraries have a meta-search engine which searches all the databases to which they have access.

Step 3: Skimming abstracts and downloading articles

Once you've settled on your search query and database, you should start to see articles that might be relevant to your topic. Rather than read every article, skim through the abstracts and see if the articles are really ones you need to read. If you like an article, make sure to download the full text PDF to your computer so you can read it later. Part of the tuition and fees your university charges you goes to paying major publishers of academic journals for the privilege of accessing their articles. Because access fees are incredibly costly, your school likely does not pay for access to all the journals in the world. While you are in school, you should never have to pay for access to an academic journal article. Instead, if your school does not subscribe to a journal you need to read, try using inter-library loan to get the article. On your university library's homepage, there is a link to inter-library loan. Just enter the information for your article (e.g. author, publication year, title), and a librarian will work with librarians at other schools to get you the PDF of the article that you need. After you leave school, getting a PDF of an article becomes more challenging. However, you can always ask an author for a copy of their article. They will usually be happy to hear someone is interested in reading and using their work.

What do you do with all of those PDFs? Some researchers keep them in folders on a cloud storage drive, arranged by topic. You may want to use a reference manager like EndNote, Mendeley, or RefWorks, which can help keep your sources and notes organized. At the very least, take notes on each article and think about how it might be of use in your study.

Step 4: Searching for author and journal names

As you scroll through the list of articles in your search results, you should begin to notice that certain authors keep appearing. If you find an author that has written multiple articles on your topic, consider searching the AUTHOR field for that particular author. You can also search the web for that author's Curriculum Vitae or CV (an academic resume) that will list their publications. Many authors maintain personal websites or host their CV on their university department's webpage. Just type in their name and "CV" into a search engine. For example, you may find Michael Sherraden's name often if your search terms are about assets and poverty. You can find his CV on the Washington University of St. Louis website.

Another way to narrow down your results is by journal name. As you are scrolling, you should also notice that many of the articles you've skimmed come from the same journals. Searching with that journal name in the JOURNAL field will allow you to narrow down your results to just that journal. For example, if you are searching for articles related to values and ethics in social work, you might want to search within the Journal of Social Work Values and Ethics. You can also navigate to the journal's webpage and browse the abstracts of the latest issues.

Step 5: Examining references

As you begin to read your articles, you'll notice that the authors cite additional articles that are likely relevant to your topic area. This is called archival searching. Unfortunately, this process will only allow you to see relevant articles from before the publication date. That is, the reference section of an article from 2014 will only have references from pre-2014. You can use Google Scholar's "cited by" feature to do a future-looking archival search. Look up an article on Google Scholar and click the "cited by" link. This is a list of all the articles that cite the article you just read. Google Scholar even allows you to search within the "cited by" articles to narrow down ones that are most relevant to your topic area. For a brief discussion about archival searching check out this article by Hammond and Brown (2008).

Step 6: Searching for systematic reviews and other sources

Another way to save time in literature searching is to look for articles that synthesize the results of other articles. Systematic reviews provide a summary of the existing literature on a topic. If you find one on your topic, you will be able to read one person's summary of the literature and go deeper by reading their references. Similarly, meta-analyses and meta-syntheses have long reference lists that are useful for finding additional sources on a topic. They use data from each article to run their own quantitative or qualitative data analysis. In this way, meta-analyses and meta-syntheses provide a more comprehensive overview of a topic. To find these kinds of articles, include the term "meta-analysis," "meta-synthesis," or "systematic review" to your search terms. Another way to find systematic reviews is through the Cochrane Collaboration or Campbell Collaboration. These institutions are dedicated to producing systematic reviews for the purposes of evidence-based practice.

Putting it all together

Familiarizing yourself with research that has already been conducted on your topic is one of the first stages of conducting a research project and is crucial for coming up with a good research design. But where to start? How to start? Earlier in this chapter you learned about some of the most common databases that house information about published social work research. As you search for literature, you may have to be fairly broad in your search for articles. Let's walk through an example. Dr. Blackstone, one of the original authors of this textbook, relates an example from her research methods class: On a college campus nearby, much to the chagrin of a group of student smokers, smoking was recently banned. These students were so upset by the idea that they would no longer be allowed to smoke on university grounds that they staged several smoke-outs during which they gathered in populated areas around campus and enjoyed a puff or two together.

A student in her research methods class wanted to understand what motivated this group of students to engage in activism centered on what she perceived to be, in this age of smoke-free facilities, a relatively deviant act. Were the protesters otherwise politically active? How much effort and coordination had it taken to organize the smoke-outs? The student researcher began her research by attempting to familiarize herself with the literature on her topic. Yet her search in Academic Search Complete for "college student activist smoke-outs," yielded no results. Concluding there was no prior research on her topic, she informed her professor that she would not be able to write the required literature review since there was no literature for her to review. How do you suppose her professor responded to this news? What went wrong with this student's search for literature?

In her first attempt, the student had been too narrow in her search for articles. But did that mean she was off the hook for completing a literature review? Absolutely not. Instead, she went back to Academic Search Complete and searched again using different combinations of search terms. Rather than searching for "college student activist smoke-outs" she tried, among other sets of terms, "college student activism." This time her search yielded a great many articles. Of course, they were not focused on pro-smoking activist efforts, but they were focused on her population of interest, college students, and on her broad topic of interest, activism. Her professor suggested that reading articles on college student activism might give her some idea about what other researchers have found in terms of what motivates college students to become involved in activist efforts. Her professor also suggested she could play around with her search terms and look for research on activism centered on other sorts of activities that are perceived by some as deviant, such as marijuana use or veganism. In other words, she needed to be broader in her search for articles.

While this student found success by broadening her search for articles, her reading of those articles needed to be narrower than her search. Once she identified a set of articles to review by searching broadly, it was time to remind herself of her specific research focus: college student activist smoke-outs. Keeping in mind her particular research interest while reviewing the literature gave her the chance to think about how the theories and findings covered in prior studies might or might not apply to her particular point of focus. For example, theories on what motivates activists to get involved might tell her something about the likely reasons the students *she* planned to study got involved. At the same time, those theories might not cover all the particulars of student participation in smoke-outs. Thinking about the different theories then gave the student the opportunity to focus her research plans and even to develop a few hypotheses about what she thought she was likely to find.

Key Takeaways

- When identifying and reading relevant literature, be broad in your search *for* articles, but be narrower in your reading *of* articles.
- Conducting a literature search involves the skillful use of keywords to find relevant articles.
- It is important to narrow down the number of articles in your search results to only those articles that are most relevant to your inquiry.

Glossary

- Query- search terms used in a database to find sources

CHAPTER TWO: READING AND EVALUATING LITERATURE

You can spend hours looking for articles online. It can be great to browse around and search on Google Scholar for articles to download and read. Unfortunately, once you have acquired a dozen or so articles you may start to feel overwhelmed that you actually have to read these articles. It certainly takes a lot of time to do it right. In this chapter, we will learn how to understand and evaluate the sources you find. We will also review how your research questions might change as you start reading in your area of interest and learn more.

Chapter outline

- 2.1 Reading an empirical journal article
- 2.2 Evaluating sources
- 2.3 Refining your question

Content advisory

This chapter discusses or mentions the following topics: sexual harassment and gender-based violence, mental health, pregnancy, and obesity.

2.1 READING AN EMPIRICAL JOURNAL ARTICLE

Learning Objectives

- Identify the key components of empirical journal articles
- Define the basic elements of the results section in a journal article
- Describe statistical significance and confidence intervals

Reading scholarly articles can be more challenging than reading a book, magazine, news article—or even some textbooks. Theoretical and practical articles are, generally speaking, easier to understand. Because empirical articles add new knowledge, they must go through great detail to demonstrate that the information they offer is based on solid science. Empirical articles can be challenging to read, and this section is designed to make that process easier for you.

Nearly all articles will have an **abstract**, the short paragraph at the beginning of an article that summarizes the author's research question, methods used to answer the question, and key findings. The abstract may also give you some idea about the theoretical perspective of the author. So, reading the abstract gives you both a framework for understanding the rest of the article and its punch line–what the author(s) found and whether the article is relevant to your area of inquiry. For this reason, it is helpful to skim abstracts as part of the literature search process.

As you will recall from Chapter 1, theoretical articles have no set structure and will look similar to reading a chapter of a book. Empirical articles contain the following sections (although exact section names vary): introduction, methods, results, and discussion. The **introduction** contains the literature review for the article and is an excellent source of information as you build your own literature review. The **methods section** reviews how the author gathered their sample, how they measured their variables, and how the data were analyzed. The **results section** provides an in-depth discussion of the findings of the study. The **discussion section** reviews the main findings and addresses how those findings fit in with the existing literature. Of course, there will also be a list of references (which you should read!) and there may be a few tables, figures, or appendices at the end of the article as well.

While you should get into the habit of familiarizing yourself with each part of the articles you wish to cite, there are strategic ways to read journal articles that can make them a little easier to digest. Once you have read the abstract for an article and determined it is one you'd like to read in full, read through the introduction and discussion sections next. Because your own review of literature is likely to emphasize findings from previous literature, you should mine the article you're reading for what's important to know about your topic. Reading the introduction helps you see the findings and articles the author considers to be significant in the topic area. Reading an article's discussion section helps you understand what the author views as their study's major findings and how the author connects those findings to other research.

In your research methods course, you pick up additional research elements that are important to understand. You learn how to identify qualitative and quantitative methods, the criteria for establishing causality, different types of causality, as well as exploratory, explanatory, and descriptive research. This textbook addresses other elements of journal articles, including choices about measurement, sampling, and design. As you learn about these additional items, you will find that the methods and results sections begin to make more sense and you will understand how the authors reached their conclusions.

As you read a research report, there are several questions you can ask yourself about each section, from abstract to conclusion. Those questions are summarized in Table 2.1. Keep in mind that the questions covered here are designed to help you, the reader, to think critically about the research you come across and to get a general understanding of the strengths, weaknesses, and key takeaways from a given study. By considering how you might respond to the following questions while reading research reports, you can gain confidence in describing the report to others and discussing its meaning and impact with them.

Table 2.1 Questions worth asking while reading research reports

Report section	Questions worth asking
Abstract	What are the key findings? How were those findings reached? What framework does the researcher employ?
Acknowledgments	Who are this study's major stakeholders? Who provided feedback? Who provided support in the form of funding or other resources?
Problem statement (introduction)	How does the author frame their research focus? What other possible ways of framing the problem exist? Why might the author have chosen this particular way of framing the problem?
Literature review (introduction)	How selective does the researcher appear to have been in identifying relevant literature to discuss? Does the review of literature appear appropriately extensive? Does the researcher provide a critical review?
Sample (methods)	Where were the data collected? Did the researcher collect their own data or use someone else's data? What population is the study trying to make claims about, and does the sample represent that population well? What are the sample's major strengths and major weaknesses?
Data collection (methods)	How were the data collected? What do you know about the relative strengths and weaknesses of the method employed? What other methods of data collection might have been employed, and why was this particular method employed? What do you know about the data collection strategy and instruments (e.g., questions asked, locations observed)? What *don't* you know about the data collection strategy and instruments?
Data analysis (methods)	How were the data analyzed? Is there enough information provided for you to feel confident that the proper analytic procedures were employed accurately?
Results	What are the study's major findings? Are findings linked back to previously described research questions, objectives, hypotheses, and literature? Are sufficient amounts of data (e.g., quotes and observations in qualitative work, statistics in quantitative work) provided in order to support conclusions drawn? Are tables readable?
Discussion/ conclusion	Does the author generalize to some population beyond her/his/their sample? How are these claims presented? Are claims made supported by data provided in the results section (e.g., supporting quotes, statistical significance)? Have limitations of the study been fully disclosed and adequately addressed? Are implications sufficiently explored?

Understanding the results section

As mentioned previously in this chapter, reading the abstract that appears in most reports of scholarly research will provide you with an excellent, easily digestible review of a study's major findings and of the framework the author is using to position their findings. Abstracts typically contain just a few hundred words, so reading them is a nice way to quickly familiarize yourself with a study. If the study seems relevant to your paper, it's probably worth reading more. If it's not, then you have only spent a minute or so reading the abstract. Another way to get a snapshot of the article is to scan the headings, tables, and figures throughout the report (Green & Simon, 2012).

One common mistake is reporting the summarized results from the abstract, rather than the detailed findings in the results section of the article. This is a problem when you are writing a literature review because you need to provide specific and clear facts that support your reading of the literature. The abstract may say something like: "we found that poverty is associated with mental health status." For your literature review, you want the details, not the summary. In the results section of the article, you may find a sentence that states: "for households in poverty, children are three times more likely to have a mental health diagnosis." This more detailed information provides a stronger basis on which to build a literature review.

Using the summarized results in an abstract is an understandable mistake to make. The results section often contains diagrams and symbols that are challenging to understand. Often, without having completed more advanced coursework on statistical or qualitative analysis, some of the terminology, symbols, or diagrams may be difficult to comprehend. To that end, the purpose of this section is to improve reading comprehension by providing an introduction to the basic components of a results section.

Journal articles often contain tables, and scanning them is a good way to begin reading an article. A **table** provides a quick, condensed summary of the report's key findings. The use of tables is not limited to one form or type of data, though they are used most commonly in quantitative research. Tables are a concise way to report large amounts of data. Some tables present descriptive information about a researcher's sample, which is often the first table in a results section. These tables will likely contain frequencies (N or n) and percentages (%). For example, if gender happened to be an important variable for the researcher's analysis, a descriptive table would show how many and what percent of all study participants are women, men, or other genders. Frequencies or "how many" will probably be listed as N or n, while the percent symbol (%) might be used to indicate percentages.

In a table presenting a causal relationship, two sets of variables are represented. The independent variable, or cause, and the dependent variable, the effect. The independent variable attributes are typically presented in the table's columns, while dependent variable attributes are presented in rows. This allows the reader to scan across a table's rows to see how values on the dependent variable attributes change as the independent variable attribute values change. Tables displaying results of quantitative analysis will also likely include some information about the strength and statistical significance of the relationships presented in the table. These details tell the reader how likely it is that the relationships presented will have occurred simply by chance.

Let's look at a specific example. Table 2.2 is based on data from a study of older workers conducted by Dr. Blackstone, an original author of this textbook. It presents the causal relationship between gender and experiencing harassing behaviors at work. In this example, gender is the independent variable (the cause) and the harassing behaviors listed are the dependent variables (the effects). [1] Therefore, we place gender in the table's columns and harassing behaviors in the table's rows.

Reading across the table's top row, we see that 2.9% of women in the sample reported experiencing subtle or obvious threats to their safety at work, while 4.7% of men in the sample reported the same. We can read across each of the rows of the table in this way. Reading across the bottom row, we see that 9.4% of women in the sample reported experiencing staring or invasion of their personal space at work while just 2.3% of men in the sample reported having the same experience. We'll discuss p-value later in this section.

Table 2.2 Percentage reporting harassing behaviors at work

Behavior Experienced at work	Women	Men	p-value
Subtle or obvious threats to your safety	2.9%	4.7%	0.623
Being hit, pushed, or grabbed	2.2%	4.7%	0.480
Comments or behaviors that demean your gender	6.5%	2.3%	0.184
Comments or behaviors that demean your age	13.8%	9.3%	0.407
Staring or invasion of your personal space	9.4%	2.3%	0.039

Note: Sample size was 138 for women and 43 for men.

These statistics represent what the researchers found in their sample, and they are using their sample to make conclusions about the true population of all employees in the real world. Because the methods we use in social science are never perfect, there is some amount of error in that value. The researchers in this study estimated the true value we would get if we asked every employee in the world the same questions on our survey. Researchers will often provide a **confidence interval**, or a range of values in which the true value is likely to be, to provide a more accurate description of their data. For example, at the time Matthew DeCarlo wrote this, his wife was expecting their first child. The doctor told them their due date was August 15th. But the doctor also told them that August 15th was only the best estimate. They were actually 95% sure the baby might be born any time between August 1st and September 1st. Confidence intervals are often listed with a percentage, like 90% or 95%, and a range of values, such as between August

1. It wouldn't make any sense to say that people's workplace experiences *cause* their gender, so in this example, the question of which is the independent variable and which are the dependent variables has a pretty obvious answer.

1st and Setptember 1st. You can read that as: we are 95% sure your baby will be born between August 1st and September 1st. So, while they got a due date of August 15th, the uncertainty about the exact date is reflected in the confidence interval provided by their doctor.

Of course, we cannot assume that these patterns didn't simply occur by chance. How confident can we be that the findings presented in the table did not occur by chance? This is where tests of statistical significance come in handy. **Statistical significance** tells us the likelihood that the relationships we observe could be caused by something other than chance. While statistics classes give you more specific details on tests of statistical significance and reading quantitative tables, the important thing to be aware of as a non-expert reader of tables is that some of the relationships presented will be statistically significant and others may not be. Tables should provide information about the statistical significance of the relationships presented. When reading a researcher's conclusions, pay attention to which relationships are statistically significant and which are not.

In Table 2.2, you may have noticed that a p value is noted in the very last column of the table. A **p-value** is a statistical measure of the probability that there is no relationship between the variables under study. Another way of putting this is that the p-value provides guidance on whether or not we should reject the null hypothesis. The **null hypothesis** is simply the assumption that no relationship exists between the variables in question. In Table 2.2, we see that for the first behavior listed, the p value is 0.623. This means that there is a 62.3% chance that the null hypothesis is correct in this case. In other words, it seems likely that any relationship between observed gender and experiencing threats to safety at work in this sample is simply due to chance.

In the final row of the table, however, we see that the p-value is 0.039. In other words, there is a 3.9% chance that the null hypothesis is correct. Thus, we can be somewhat more confident than in the preceding example that there may be some relationship between a person's gender and their experiencing the behavior noted in this row. Statistical significance is reported in reference to a value, usually 0.05 in the social science. This means that the probability that the relationship between gender and experiencing staring or invasion of personal space at work is due to random chance is less than 5 in 100. Social science often uses 0.05, but other values are used. Studies using 0.1 are using a more forgiving standard of significance, and therefore, have a higher likelihood of error (10%). Studies using 0.01 are using a more stringent standard of significance, and therefore, have a lower likelihood of error (1%).

Notice being conservative by using words like *somewhat* and *may be*. When testing hypotheses, social scientists generally phrase their findings in terms of rejecting the null hypothesis rather than making bold statements about the relationships observed in their tables. You can learn more about creating tables, reading tables, and tests of statistical significance in a class focused exclusively on statistical analysis. For now,this brief introduction to reading tables may improve your confidence in reading and understanding the quantitative tables you encounter while reading reports of social science research.

A final caveat is worth noting here. The previous discussion applies to *quantitative* articles. Quantitative articles will contain a lot of numbers and the results of statistical tests demonstrating association between those numbers. As a result, they usually have tables and report statistics. *Qualitative* articles, on the other hand, will consist mostly of quotations from participants. For most qualitative articles, the authors want to put their results in the words of their participants, as they are the experts. The results section may be organized by theme, with each paragraph or subsection illustrating through quotes how the authors interpret what people in their study said.

Key Takeaways

- Reading a research article requires reading beyond the abstract.
- In tables presenting causal relationships, the independent variable is typically presented in the table's columns while the dependent variables are presented in the table's rows.
- When reading a research report, there are several key questions you should ask yourself for each section of the report.

Glossary

- Abstract- the short paragraph at the beginning of an article that summarizes the its main point
- Confidence interval- a range of values in which the true value is likely to be
- Null hypothesis- the assumption that no relationship exists between the variables in question
- *p*-value- a statistical measure of the probability that there is no relationship between the variables under study
- Statistical significance- the likelihood that the relationships that are observed could be caused by something other than chance
- Table- a quick, condensed summary of the report's key findings

Image Attributions

CSAF releases 2009 reading list by Master Sgt. Steven Goetsch public domain

2.2 EVALUATING SOURCES

Learning Objectives
• Critically evaluate the sources of the information you have found • Apply the information from each source to your research proposal • Identify how to be a responsible consumer of research

In Chapter 1, you developed a "working question" to guide your inquiry and learned how to use online databases to find sources. By now, you've hopefully collected a number of academic journal articles relevant to your topic area. It's now time to evaluate the information you found. Not only do you want to be sure of the source and the quality of the information, but you also want to determine whether each item is an appropriate fit for your literature review.

This is also the point at which you make sure you have searched for and obtained publications for all areas of your research question and that you go back into the literature for another search, if necessary. You may also want to consult with your professor or the syllabus for your class to see what is expected for your literature review.

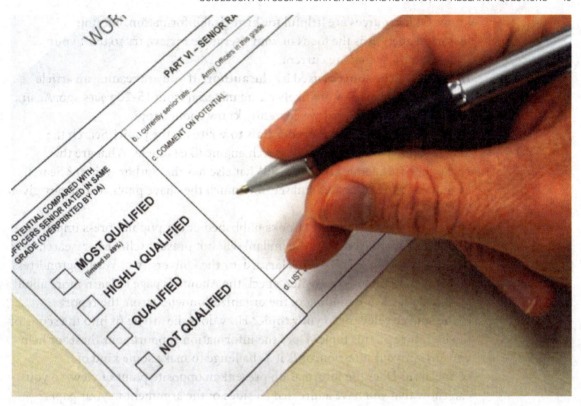

It is likely that most of the resources you locate for your review will be from the scholarly literature of your discipline or in your topic area. As we have already seen, peer-reviewed articles are written by and for experts in a field. They generally describe formal research studies or experiments with the purpose of providing insight on a topic. You may have located these articles through the four databases in Chapter 1 or through archival searching. You now may want to know how to evaluate the usefulness for your research.

In general, when we discuss evaluation of sources, we are talking about quality, accuracy, relevance, bias, reputation, currency, and credibility factors in a specific work, whether it's a book, ebook, article, website, or blog posting. Before you include a source in your literature review, you should clearly understand what it is and why you are including it. According to Bennard et al. (2014), "Using inaccurate, irrelevant, or poorly researched sources can affect the quality of your own work" (para. 4). When evaluating a work for inclusion in, or exclusion from, your literature review, ask yourself a series of questions about each source.

1. **Is the information outdated?** Is the source more than 5-10 years old? If so, it will not provide what we currently know about the topic–just what we used to

know. Older sources are helpful for historical information, but unless historical analysis is the focus of your literature review, try to limit your sources to those that are current.

2. **How old are the sources used by the author?** If you are reading an article from 10 years ago, they are likely citing material from 15-20 years ago. Again, this does not reflect what we currently know about a topic.

3. **Does the author have the credentials to write on the topic?** Search the author's name in a general web search engine like Google. What are the researcher's academic credentials? What else has this author written? Search by author in the databases and see how much they have published on any given subject.

4. **Who published the source?** Books published under popular press imprints (such as Random House or Macmillan) will not present scholarly research in the same way as Sage, Oxford, Harvard, or the University of Washington Press. For grey literature and websites, check the About Us page to learn more about potential biases and funding of the organization who wrote the report.

5. **Is the source relevant to your topic?** How does the article fit into the scope of the literature on this topic? Does the information support your thesis or help you answer your question, or is it a challenge to make some kind of connection? Does the information present an opposite point of view, so you can show that you have addressed all sides of the argument in your paper? Many times, literature searches will include articles that ultimately are not that relevant to your final topic. You don't need to read everything!

6. **How important is this source in the literature?** If you search for the article on Google Scholar (see Figure 3.1 for an example of a search result from Google Scholar), you can see how many other sources cited this information. Generally, the higher the number of citations, the more important the article. This is a way to find seminal articles – "A classic work of research literature that is more than 5 years old and is marked by its uniqueness and contribution to professional knowledge" (Houser, 2018, p. 112).

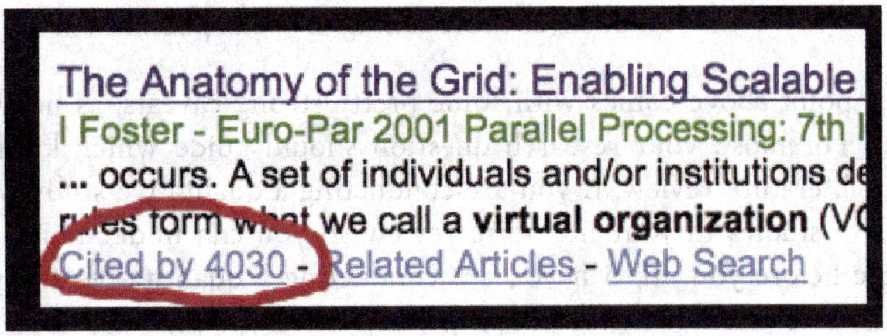

The Anatomy of the Grid: Enabling Scalable
I Foster - Euro-Par 2001 Parallel Processing: 7th I
... occurs. A set of individuals and/or institutions de
rules form what we call a **virtual organization** (VC
Cited by 4030 - Related Articles - Web Search

Figure 2.1 Google Scholar

1

7. **Is the source accurate?** Check the facts in the article. Can statistics be verified through other sources? Does this information seem to fit with what you have read in other sources?

8. **Is the source reliable and objective?** Is a particular point of view or bias immediately obvious, or does it seem objective at first glance? What point of view does the author represent? Are they clear about their point of view? Is the article an editorial that is trying to argue a position? Is the article in a publication with a particular editorial position?

9. **What is the scope of the article?** Is it a general work that provides an overview of the topic or is it specifically focused on only one aspect of your topic?

10. **How strong is the evidence in the article?** What are the research methods used in the article? Where does the method fall in the hierarchy of evidence?

- Meta-analysis and meta-synthesis: a systematic and scientific review that uses quantitative or qualitative methods (respectively) to summarize the results of many studies on a topic.
- Experiments and quasi-experiments: include a group of patients in an experimental group, as well as a control group. These groups are monitored for the variables/outcomes of interest. Randomized control trials are the gold standard.
- Longitudinal surveys: follow a group of people to identify how variables of interest change over time.
- Cross-sectional surveys: observe individuals at one point in time and discover relationships between variables.
- Qualitative studies: use in-depth interviews and analysis of texts to

---

1. Figure 2.1 "The anatomy of the grid" was created by Palreeparit, I. (2008). Shared under a CC BY-NC 2.0 license.

uncover the meaning of social phenomena

The last point above comes with some pretty strong caveats, as no study is really *better* than another. Foremost, your research question should guide which kinds of studies you collect for your literature review. If you are conducting a qualitative study, you should include some qualitative studies in your literature review so you can understand how others have studied the topic before you. Even if you are conducting a quantitative study, qualitative research is important for understanding processes and the lived experience of people. Any article that demonstrates rigor in thought and methods is appropriate to use in your inquiry.

At the beginning of a project, you may not know what kind of research project you will ultimately propose. It is at this point that consulting a meta-analysis, meta-synthesis, or systematic review might be especially helpful as these articles try to summarize an entire body of literature into one article. Every type of source listed here is reputable, but some have greater explanatory power than others.

Thinking about your project

Thinking about the overarching goals of your research project and finding and reviewing the existing literature on your topic are two of the initial steps you'll take when designing a research project. Forming a working research question, as discussed in section 1.1, is another crucial step. Creating and refining your research question will help you identify the key concepts you will study. Once you have identified those concepts, you'll need to decide how to define them, and how you'll *know* that you're observing them when it comes time to collect your data. Defining your concepts, and knowing them when you see them, relates to conceptualization and operationalization. Of course, you also need to know what approach you will take to collect your data. Thus, identifying your research method is another important part of research design.

You also need to think about who your research participants will be and what larger group(s) they may represent. Last, but certainly not least, you should consider any potential ethical concerns that could arise during the course of your research project. These concerns might come up during your data collection, but they might also arise when you get to the point of analyzing or sharing your research results.

Decisions about the various research components do not necessarily occur in sequential order. In fact, you may have to think about potential ethical concerns even before zeroing in on a specific research question. Similarly, the goal of being able to make generalizations about your population of interest could shape the decisions you make about your method of data collection. Putting it all together, the following list shows some of the major components you'll need to consider as you design your research project. Make sure you have information that will help inform how you think about each component.

- Research question
- Literature review
- Research strategy (idiographic or nomothetic, inductive or deductive)
- Units of analysis and units of observation
- Key concepts (conceptualization and operationalization)
- Method of data collection
- Research participants (sample and population)
- Ethical concerns

Being a responsible consumer of research

Being a responsible consumer of research requires you to take seriously your identity as a social scientist. Now that you are familiar with how to conduct research and how to read the results of others' research, you have some responsibility to put your knowledge and skills to use. Doing so is in part a matter of being able to distinguish what you do know based on the information provided by research findings from what you do not know. It is also a matter of having some awareness about what you can and cannot reasonably know as you encounter research findings.

When assessing social scientific findings, think about what information has been provided to you. In a scholarly journal article, you will presumably be given a great deal of information about the researcher's method of data collection, her sample, and information about how the researcher identified and recruited research participants. All of these details provide important contextual information that can help you assess the researcher's claims. If, on the other hand, you come across some discussion of social scientific research in a popular magazine or newspaper, chances are that you will not find the same level of detailed information that you would find in a scholarly journal article. In this case, what you do and do not know is more limited than in the case of a scholarly journal article. If the research appears in popular media, search for the author or study title in an academic database.

Also, take into account whatever information is provided about a study's funding source. Most funders want, and in fact require, that recipients acknowledge them in publications. But more popular press may leave out a funding source. In this Internet age, it can be relatively easy to obtain information about how a study was funded. If this information is not provided in the source from which you learned about a study, it might behoove you to do a quick search on the web to see if you can learn more about a researcher's funding. Findings that seem to support a particular political agenda, for example, might have more or less weight once you know whether and by whom a study was funded.

There is some information that even the most responsible consumer of research cannot know. Because researchers are ethically bound to protect the identities of their subjects, for example, we will never know exactly who participated in a given study. Researchers may also choose not to reveal any personal stakes they hold in the research they conduct. While researchers may "start where they are," we cannot know for certain whether or how researchers are personally connected to their work unless they choose to share such details. Neither of these "unknowables" is necessarily problematic, but having some awareness of what you may never know about a study does provide important contextual information from which to assess what one can "take away" from a given report of findings.

Key Takeaways

- Not all published articles are the same. Evaluating sources requires a careful investigation of each source.
- Being a responsible consumer of research means giving serious thought to and understanding what you do know, what you don't know, what you can know, and what you can't know.

2.3 REFINING YOUR QUESTION

Learning Objectives

- Develop and revise questions that focus your inquiry
- Create a concept map that demonstrates the relationships between concepts

Once you have selected your topic area and reviewed literature related to it, you may need to narrow it to something that can be realistically researched and answered. In the last section, we learned about asking who, what, when, where, why, and how questions. As you read more about your topic area you the focus of your inquiry should become more specific and clear. As a result, you might begin to ask to begin to ask questions that describe a phenomenon, compare one phenomenon with another, or probe the relationship between two concepts.

You might begin by asking a series of **PICO** questions. Although the PICO method is used primarily in the health sciences, it can also be useful for narrowing/refining a research question in the social sciences as well. A way to formulate an answerable question using the PICO model could look something like this:

- **Patient, population or problem:** What are the characteristics of the patient or population? (e.g., gender, age, other demographics) What is the social problem or diagnosis you are interested in? (e.g., poverty or substance use disorder)
- **Intervention or exposure:** What do you want to do with the patient, person, or population (e.g., treat, diagnose, observe)? For example, you may want to observe a client's behavior or a reaction to a specific type of treatment.
- **Comparison:** What is the alternative to the intervention? (e.g., other therapeutic interventions, programs, or policies) For example, how does a sample group that is assigned to mandatory rehabilitation compare to an intervention that builds motivation to enter treatment voluntarily?

- **Outcome:** What are the relevant outcomes? (e.g., academic achievement, healthy relationships, shame) For example, how does recognizing triggers for trauma flashbacks impact the target population?

Some examples of how the PICO method is used to refine a research question include:

- "Can music therapy help autistic students improve their communication skills?"
  - ∘ Population (autistic students)
  - ∘ Intervention (music therapy)
- "How effective are antidepressant medications on anxiety and depression?"
  - ∘ Population (clients with anxiety and depression)
  - ∘ Intervention (antidepressants)
- "How does race impact help-seeking for students with mental health diagnoses?
  - ∘ Population (students with mental health diagnoses, students of minority races)
  - ∘ Comparison (students of different races)
  - ∘ Outcome (seeking help for mental health issues)

Another mnemonic technique used in the social sciences for narrowing a topic is **SPICE**. An example of how SPICE factors can be used to develop a research question is given below:

- **S**etting – for example, a college campus
- **P**erspective – for example, college students
- **I**ntervention – for example, text message reminders
- **C**omparisons – for example, telephone message reminders
- **E**valuation – for example, number of cigarettes used after text message reminder compared to the number of cigarettes used after a telephone reminder

Developing a concept map

Likewise, developing a concept map or mind map around your topic may help you analyze your question and determine more precisely what you want to research. Using this technique, start with the broad topic, issue, or problem, and begin writing down all the words, phrases and ideas related to that topic that come to mind and then 'map' them to the original idea. This technique is illustrated in Figure 2.2.

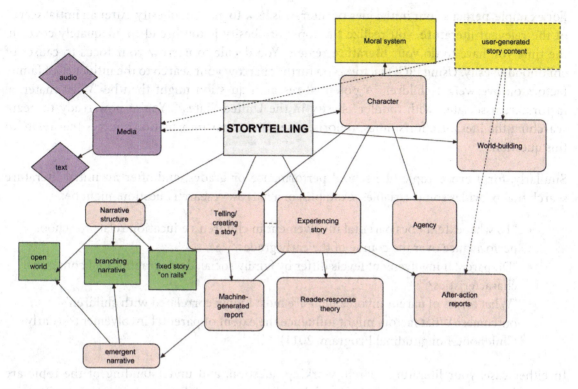

Figure 2.2 Basic concept map

1

Concept mapping aims to improve the "description of the breadth and depth of literature in a domain of inquiry. It also facilitates identification of the number and nature of studies underpinning mapped relationships among concepts, thus laying the groundwork for systematic research reviews and meta-analyses" (Lesley, Floyd, & Oermann, 2002, p. 229). Its purpose, like the other methods of question refining, is to help you organize, prioritize, and integrate material into a workable research area; one that is interesting, answerable, feasible, objective, scholarly, original, and clear.

In addition to helping you get started with your own literature review, the concept mapping will give you some keywords and concepts that will be useful when you begin searching the literature for relevant studies and publications on your topic. Concept mapping can also be helpful when creating a topical outline or drafting your literature review, as it demonstrates the important of each concept and sub-concepts as well as the relationships between each concept.

1. Figure 2.2 image "gaming and narrative discussion" created by Bryan Alexander (2012). Shared under a CC-BY 2.0 license

For example, perhaps your initial idea or interest is how to prevent obesity. After an initial search of the relevant literature, you realize the topic of obesity is too broad to adequately cover in the time you have to do your literature review. You decide to narrow your focus to causes of childhood obesity. Using PICO factors, you further narrow your search to the influence of family factors on overweight children. A potential research question might then be "What maternal factors are associated with toddler obesity in the United States?" You're now ready to begin searching the literature for studies, reports, cases, and other information sources that relate to this question.

Similarly, for a broad topic like school performance or grades, and after an initial literature search that provides some variables, examples of a narrow research question might be:

- "To what extent does parental involvement in children's education relate to school performance over the course of the early grades?"
- "Do parental involvement levels differ by family social, demographic, and contextual characteristics?"
- "What forms of parent involvement are most highly correlated with children's outcomes? What factors might influence the extent of parental involvement?" (Early Childhood Longitudinal Program, 2011).

In either case, your literature search, working question, and understanding of the topic are constantly changing as your knowledge of the topic deepens. A literature review is an iterative process, one that stops, starts, and loops back on itself multiple times before completion. As research is a practice behavior of social workers, you should apply the same type of critical reflection to your inquiry as you would to your clinical or macro practice.

Key Takeaways

- As you read more articles, you should revise your original question to make it more focused and clear.
- You can further develop the important concepts and relationships for your project by using concept maps and the PICO/SPICE frameworks.

CHAPTER THREE: CONDUCTING A LITERATURE REVIEW

Whether you plan to engage in clinical, administrative, or policy practice, all social workers must be able to look at the available literature on a topic and synthesize the relevant facts into a coherent review. Literature reviews can have a powerful effect, for example, by providing the factual basis for a new program or policy in an agency or government. In your own research proposal, conducting a thorough literature review will help you build strong arguments for why your topic is important and why your research question must be answered.

Chapter outline

- 3.1 What is a literature review?
- 3.2 Synthesizing literature
- 3.3 Writing the literature review

Content advisory

This chapter discusses or mentions the following topics: homelessness, suicide, depression, LGBTQ oppression, drug use, and psychotic disorders.

3.1 WHAT IS A LITERATURE REVIEW?

CHAPTER THREE: CONDUCTING A
LITERATURE REVIEW

Learning Objectives

- Describe the components of a literature review
- Recognize commons errors in literature reviews

Pick up nearly any book on research methods and you will find a description of a **literature review**. At a basic level, the term implies a survey of factual or nonfiction books, articles, and other documents published on a particular subject. Definitions may be similar across the disciplines, with new types and definitions continuing to emerge. Generally speaking, a literature review is a:

- "comprehensive background of the literature within the interested topic area" (O'Gorman & MacIntosh, 2015, p. 31).
- "critical component of the research process that provides an in-depth analysis of recently published research findings in specifically identified areas of interest" (Houser, 2018, p. 109).
- "written document that presents a logically argued case founded on a comprehensive understanding of the current state of knowledge about a topic of study" (Machi & McEvoy, 2012, p. 4).

Literature reviews are indispensable for academic research. "A substantive, thorough, sophisticated literature review is a precondition for doing substantive, thorough, sophisticated research...A researcher cannot perform significant research without first understanding the literature in the field" (Boote & Beile, 2005, p. 3). In the literature review, a researcher shows she is familiar with a body of knowledge and thereby establishes her credibility with a reader. The literature review shows how previous research is linked to the author's project, summarizing and synthesizing what is known while identifying gaps in the knowledge base, facilitating theory development, closing areas where enough research already exists, and uncovering areas where more research is needed. (Webster & Watson, 2002, p. xiii). They are often necessary for real world social work practice. Grant proposals, advocacy briefs, and evidence-based practice rely on a review of the literature to accomplish practice goals.

A literature review is a compilation of the most significant previously published research on your topic. Unlike an annotated bibliography or a research paper you may have written in other classes, your literature review will outline, evaluate, and synthesize relevant research and relate those sources to your own research question. It is much more than a summary of all the related literature. A good literature review lays the foundation for the importance of the problem your research project addresses defines the main ideas in your research question and their interrelationships.

Literature review basics

All literature reviews, whether they focus on qualitative or quantitative data, will at some point:
1. Introduce the topic and define its key terms.
2. Establish the importance of the topic.
3. Provide an overview of the important literature on the concepts in the research question and other related concepts.
4. Identify gaps in the literature or controversies.
5. Point out consistent finding across studies.
6. Arrive at a synthesis that organizes what is known about a topic, rather than just summarizing.
7. Discusses possible implications and directions for future research.

There are many different types of literature reviews, including those that focus solely on methodology, those that are more conceptual, and those that are more exploratory. Regardless of the type of literature review or how many sources it contains, strong literature reviews have similar characteristics. Your literature review is, at its most fundamental level, an original work based on an extensive critical examination and synthesis of the relevant literature on a topic. As a study of the research on a particular topic, it is arranged by key themes or findings, which should lead up to or link to the research question.

A literature review is a mandatory part of any research project. It demonstrates that you can systematically explore the research in your topic area, read and analyze the literature on the topic, use it to inform your own work, and gather enough knowledge about the topic to conduct a research project. Literature reviews should be reasonably complete, and not restricted to a few journals, a few years, or a specific methodology or research design. A well-conducted literature review should indicate to you whether your initial research questions have already been addressed in the literature, whether there are newer or more interesting research questions available, and whether the original research questions should be modified or changed in light of findings of the literature review. The review can also provide some intuitions or potential answers to the questions of interest and/or help identify theories that have previously been used to address similar questions and may provide evidence to inform policy or decision-making (Bhattacherjee, 2012).

Literature reviews are also beneficial to you as a researcher and scholar in social work. By reading what others have argued and found in their work, you become familiar with how people talk about and understand your topic. You will also refine your writing skills and your understanding of the topic you have chosen. The literature review also impacts the question you want to answer. As you learn more about your topic, you will clarify and redefine the research question guiding your inquiry. Literature reviews make sure you are not "reinventing the wheel" by repeating a study done so many times before or making an obvious error that others have encountered. The contribution your research study will have depends on what others have found before you. Try to place the study you wish to do in the context of previous research and ask, "Is this contributing something new?" and "Am I addressing a gap in knowledge or controversy in the literature?"

In summary, you should conduct a literature review to:

- Locate gaps in the literature of your discipline
- Avoid "reinventing the wheel"
- Carry on the unfinished work of other scholars
- Identify other people working in the same field
- Increase breadth and depth of knowledge in your subject area
- Read the seminal works in your field
- Provide intellectual context for your own work
- Acknowledge opposing viewpoints
- Put your work in perspective
- Demonstrate you can find and understand previous work in the area

Common literature review errors

Literature reviews are more than a summary of the publications you find on a topic. As you have seen in this brief introduction, literature reviews are a very specific type of research, analysis, and writing. We will explore these topics more in the next chapters. As you begin your literature review, here are some common errors to avoid:

- Accepting another researcher's finding as valid without evaluating methodology and data
- Ignoring contrary findings and alternative interpretations
- Using findings that are not clearly related to your own study or using findings that are too general
- Dedicating insufficient time to literature searching
- Simply reporting isolated statistical results, rather than synthesizing the results
- Relying too heavily on secondary sources
- Overusing quotations from sources
- Not justifying arguments using specific facts or theories from the literature

For a quick review of some of the pitfalls and challenges a new researcher faces when she begins work, see "Get Ready: Academic Writing, General Pitfalls and (oh yes) Getting Started!".

Key Takeaways

- Literature reviews are the first step in any research project, as they help you learn about the topic you chose to study.
- You must do more than summarize sources for a literature review. You must have something to say about them and demonstrate you understand their content.

Glossary

- Literature review- a survey of factual or nonfiction books, articles, and other documents published on a particular subject

---

Image attributions

Book library by MVA CC-0

3.2 SYNTHESIZING LITERATURE

Learning Objectives

- Connect the sources you read with key concepts in your research question and proposal
- Systematize the information and facts from each source you read

Putting the pieces together

Combining separate elements into a whole is the dictionary definition of synthesis. It is a way to make connections among and between numerous and varied source materials. A literature review is not an annotated bibliography, organized by title, author, or date of publication. Rather, it is grouped by topic and argument to create a whole view of the literature relevant to your research question.

Your synthesis must demonstrate a critical analysis of the papers you collected, as well as your ability to integrate the results of your analysis into your own literature review. Each source you collect should be critically evaluated and weighed based on the criteria from Chapter 2 before you include it in your review.

Begin the synthesis process by creating a grid, table, or an outline where you will summarize your literature review findings, using common themes you have identified and the sources you have found. The summary, grid, or outline will help you compare and contrast the themes, so you can see the relationships among them as well as areas where you may need to do more searching. A basic summary table is provided in Figure 3.2. Whichever method you choose, this type of organization will help you to both understand the information you find and structure the writing of your review. Remember, although "the means of summarizing can vary, the key at this point is to make sure you understand what you've found and how it relates to your topic and research question" (Bennard et al., 2014, para. 10).

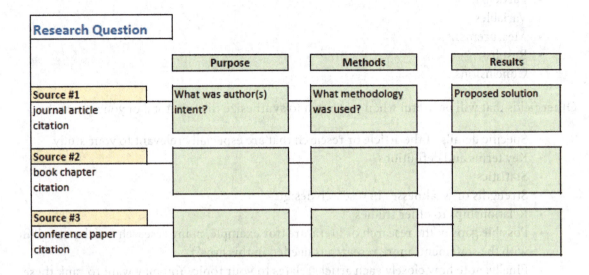

Figure 3.2 Summary table

1

As you read through the material you gather, look for common themes as they may provide the structure for your literature review. And, remember, writing a literature review is an iterative process. It is not unusual to go back and search academic databases for more sources of information as you read the articles you've collected.

Literature reviews can be organized sequentially or by topic, theme, method, results, theory, or argument. It's important to develop categories that are meaningful and relevant to your research question. Take detailed notes on each article and use a consistent format for capturing all the information each article provides. These notes and the summary table can be done manually using note cards. However, given the amount of information you will be recording, an electronic file created in a word processing or spreadsheet (like this example Literature Search Template) is more manageable. Examples of fields you may want to capture in your notes include:

- Authors' names
- Article title
- Publication year
- Main purpose of the article
- Methodology or research design

1. Figure 3.2 copied from Frederiksen, L. & Phelps, S. F. (2018). Literature reviews for education and nursing graduate students. Shared under a CC-BY 4.0 license.

- Participants
- Variables
- Measurement
- Results
- Conclusions

Other fields that will be useful when you begin to synthesize the sum total of your research:

- Specific details of the article or research that are especially relevant to your study
- Key terms and definitions
- Statistics
- Strengths or weaknesses in research design
- Relationships to other studies
- Possible gaps in the research or literature (for example, many research articles conclude with the statement "more research is needed in this area")
- Finally, note how closely each article relates to your topic. You may want to rank these as high, medium, or low relevance. For papers that you decide not to include, you may want to note your reasoning for exclusion, such as small sample size, local case study, or lacks evidence to support conclusions.

An example of how to organize summary tables by author or theme is shown in Table 3.1.

Table 3.1: Summary table

Author/ Year	Research Design	Participants or Population Studied	Comparison	Outcome
Smith/2010	Mixed methods	Undergraduates	Graduates	Improved access
King/2016	Survey	Females	Males	Increased representation
Miller/ 2011	Content analysis	Nurses	Doctors	New procedure

Here is an example summary table template.

Creating a topical outline

An alternative way to organize your articles for synthesis it to create an outline. After you have collected the articles you intend to use (and have put aside the ones you won't be using), it's time to extract as much as possible from the facts provided in those articles. You are starting your research project without a lot of hard facts on the topics you want to study, and by using the literature reviews provided in academic journal articles, you can gain a lot of knowledge about a topic in a short period of time.

As you read an article in detail, try copying the information you find relevant to your research topic in a separate word processing document. Copying and pasting from PDF to Word can be a pain because PDFs are image files not documents. To make that easier, use the HTML version of the article, convert the PDF to Word in Adobe Acrobat or another PDF reader, or use "paste special" command to paste the content into Word without formatting. If it's an old PDF, you may have to simply type  out the information you need. It can be a messy job, but having all of your facts in one place is very helpful for drafting your literature review. Of course, you will not be using other authors' words in your own literature review, but this is a good way to start compiling your notes.

You should copy and paste any fact or argument you consider important. Some good examples include definitions of concepts, statistics about the size of the social problem, and empirical evidence about the key variables in the research question, among countless others. It's a good idea to consult with your professor and the syllabus for the course about what they are looking for when they read your literature review. Facts for your literature review are principally found in the introduction, results, and discussion section of an empirical article or at any point in a non-empirical article. Copy and paste into your notes anything you may want to use in your literature review.

Importantly, you must make sure you note the original source of that information. Nothing is worse than searching your articles for hours only to realize you forgot to note where your facts came from. If you found a statistic that the author used in the introduction, it almost certainly came from another source that the author cited in a footnote or internal citation. You will want to check the original source to make sure the author represented the information correctly. Moreover, you may want to read the original study to learn more about your topic and discover other sources relevant to your inquiry.

Assuming you have pulled all of the facts out of multiple articles, it's time to start thinking about how these pieces of information relate to each other. Start grouping each fact into categories and subcategories as shown in Figure 3.3. For example, a statistic stating that homeless single adults are more likely to be male may fit into a category of gender and homelessness. For each topic or subtopic you identified during your critical analysis of each paper, determine what those papers have in common. Likewise, determine which ones in the group differ. If there are contradictory findings, you may be able to identify methodological or theoretical differences that could account for the contradiction. For example, one study may sample only high-income earners or those in a rural area. Determine what general conclusions you can report about the topic or subtopic, based on all of the information you've found.

Create a separate document containing a topical outline that combines your facts from each source and organizes them by topic or category. As you include more facts and more sources into your topical outline, you will begin to see how each fact fits into a category and how categories are related to each other. Your category names may change over time, as may their definitions. This is a natural reflection of the learning you are doing.

Table 3.2 Topical outline[2]

Facts copied from an article	Topical outline: Facts organized by category
• Accumulating evidence indicates that adolescents who have same-sex sexual attractions, who have had sexual or romantic relationships with persons of the same sex, or who identify as lesbian, gay, or bisexual are more likely than heterosexual adolescents to experience depressive symptoms, suicidal ideation, and to make suicide attempts (Remafedi et al. 1998; Russell and Joyner 2001; Safren and Heimberg 1999).	**LGB adolescents and suicide** • Accumulating evidence indicates that adolescents who have same-sex sexual attractions, who have had sexual or romantic relationships with persons of the same sex, or who identify as lesbian, gay, or bisexual are more likely than heterosexual adolescents to experience depressive symptoms, suicidal ideation, and to make suicide attempts (Remafedi et al. 1998; Russell and Joyner 2001; Safren and Heimberg 1999).
• Youth Risk Behavior Surveillance (YRBS) system showed that 40% of youth who reported a minority sexual orientation indicated feeling sad or hopeless in the past 2 weeks, compared to 26% of heterosexual youth (District of Columbia Public Schools, 2007). Those data also showed that lesbian, gay, and bisexual youth were more than twice as likely as heterosexual youth to have considered attempting suicide in the past year (31% vs. 14%). This body of research demonstrates that lesbian, gay, and bisexual youth have high levels of emotional distress.	**LGB adolescents and emotional distress** • Youth Risk Behavior Surveillance (YRBS) system showed that 40% of youth who reported a minority sexual orientation indicated feeling sad or hopeless in the past 2 weeks, compared to 26% of heterosexual youth (District of Columbia Public Schools, 2007). Those data also showed that lesbian, gay, and bisexual youth were more than twice as likely as heterosexual youth to have considered attempting suicide in the past year (31% vs. 14%). This body of research demonstrates that lesbian, gay, and bisexual youth have high levels of emotional distress.

2. This table was adapted from the work of Amanda Parsons

	Transgender adolescents and emotional distress
• A much smaller body of research suggests that adolescents who identify as transgendered or transsexual also experience increased emotional distress (Di Ceglie et al. 2002; Grossman and D'Augelli 2006, 2007). • In a study based on a convenience sample of 55 transgendered youth aged to 15–21 years, the authors found that more than one fourth reported a prior suicide attempt (Grossman and D'Augelli 2007).	• A much smaller body of research suggests that adolescents who identify as transgendered or transsexual also experience increased emotional distress (Di Ceglie et al. 2002; Grossman and D'Augelli 2006, 2007). • In a study based on a convenience sample of 55 transgendered youth aged to 15–21 years, the authors found that more than one fourth reported a prior suicide attempt (Grossman and D'Augelli 2007).

A complete topical outline is a long list of facts, arranged by category about your topic. As you step back from the outline, you should understand the topic areas where you have enough information to make strong conclusions about what the literature says. You should also assess in what areas you need to do more research before you can write a robust literature review. The topical outline should serve as a transitional document between the notes you write on each source and the literature review you submit to your professor. It is important to note that they contain plagiarized information that is copied and pasted directly from the primary sources. That's okay because these are just notes and are not meant to be turned in as your own ideas. For your final literature review, you must paraphrase these sources to avoid plagiarism. More importantly, you should keep your voice and ideas front-and-center in what you write as this is *your* analysis of the literature. Make strong claims and support them thoroughly using facts you found in the literature. We will pick up the task of writing your literature review in section 3.3.

Additional resources for synthesizing literature

There are many ways to approach synthesizing literature. We've reviewed two examples here: summary tables and topical outlines. Other examples you may encounter include annotated bibliographies and synthesis matrices. As you are learning research, find a method that works for you. Reviewing the literature is a core component of evidence-based practice in social work at any level. See the resources below if you need some additional help:

Literature Reviews: Using a Matrix to Organize Research / Saint Mary's University of Minnesota

Literature Review: Synthesizing Multiple Sources / Indiana University

Writing a Literature Review and Using a Synthesis Matrix / Florida International University

Sample Literature Reviews Grid / Complied by Lindsay Roberts

Killam, Laura (2013). *Literature review preparation: Creating a summary table.* Includes transcript.

Key Takeaways

- It is necessary to take notes on research articles as you read. Try to develop a system that works for you to keep your notes organized, such as a summary table.
- Summary tables and topical outlines help researchers synthesize sources for the purpose of writing a literature review.

Image attributions

Pieces of the puzzle by congerdesign CC-0

Adult diary by Pexels CC-0

3.3 WRITING THE LITERATURE REVIEW

Congratulations! By now, you should have discovered, retrieved, evaluated, synthesized, and organized the information you need for your literature review. It's now time to turn that stack of articles, papers, and notes into a literature review–it's time to start writing!

If you've followed the steps in this chapter, you likely have an outline from which you can begin the writing process. But what do you need to include in your literature review? We've mentioned it before here, but just to summarize, a literature review should:

> …clearly describe the questions that are being asked. They also locate the research within the ongoing scholarly dialogue. This is done by summarizing current understandings and by discussing why what we already knows leads to the need for the present research. Literature reviews also define the primary concepts. While this information can appear in any order, these are the elements in all literature reviews. (Loseke, 2017, p. 61)

Do you have enough facts and sources to accomplish these tasks? It's a good time to consult your outlines and notes on each article you plan to include in your literature review. You may also want to consult with your professor on what they expect from you. If there is something that you are missing, you may want to jump back to section 2.3 where we discussed how to search for literature on your topic. While you can always fill in material later, there is always the danger that you will start writing without really knowing what you are talking about or what you want to say. For example, if you don't have a solid definition of your key concepts or a sense of how the literature has developed over time, it will be difficult to make coherent scholarly claims about your topic.

There is no magical point at which everyone is ready to write. As you consider whether you are ready or not, it may be useful to ask yourself these questions:

- How will my literature review be organized?
- What section headings will I be using?
- How do the various studies relate to each other?
- What contributions do they make to the field?
- What are the limitations of a study/where are the gaps in the research?
- And finally, but most importantly, how does my own research fit into what has already been done?

The problem statement

Many scholarly works begin with a problem statement. The problem statement serves two functions. On one hand, it establishes why your topic is a social problem worth studying. At the same time, it also pulls your reader into the literature review. Who would want to read about something unimportant?

A problem statement generally answers the following questions, though these are far from exhaustive:

- Why is this an important problem to study?
- How many people are affected by the problem?
- How does this problem impact other social issues or target populations relevant to social work?
- Why is your target population an important one to study?

A strong problem statement, like the rest of your literature review, should be filled with facts, theory, and arguments based on the literature you've found. A research proposal differs significantly from other more reflective essays you've likely completed during your social work studies. If your topic were domestic violence in rural Appalachia in the United States, you could come up with answers to the above questions without looking at a single source. However, the purpose of the literature review is not to test your intuition, personal experience, or empathy. Instead, research methods are about learning specific and articulate-able facts to inform social work action. With a problem statement, you can take a "boring" topic like the color of rooms used in an inpatient psychiatric facility, transportation patterns in major cities, or the materials used to manufacture baby bottles and help others see the topic as you see it—an important part of the social world that impacts social work practice.

The structure of a literature review

The problem statement generally belongs at the beginning of the literature review. Take care not to go on for too long. A good rule of thumb is to spend no more than a paragraph or two for a problem statement. For the rest of your literature review, there is no set formula for how it should be organized. However, a literature review generally follows the format of any other essay—Introduction, Body, and Conclusion.

The introduction to the literature review contains a statement or statements about the overall topic. At minimum, the introduction should define or identify the general topic, issue, or area of concern. You might consider presenting historical background, mention the results of a seminal study, and provide definitions of important terms. The introduction may also point to overall trends in what has been previously published on the topic or conflicts in theory, methodology, evidence, conclusions, or gaps in research and scholarship. Put in a few sentences that walk the reader through the rest of the literature review. Highlight your main arguments from the body of the literature review and preview your conclusion. An introduction should let someone know what to expect from the rest of your review.

The body of your literature review is where you demonstrate your synthesis and analysis of the literature on your topic. Again, take care not to just summarize your literature. It's not a good idea to organize your literature review by source—that is, one paragraph for source A, one paragraph for source B, etc. That structure will likely provide an okay summary of the literature you've found, but it would give you almost no synthesis of the literature. That approach doesn't tell your reader how to put those facts together, points of agreement or contention in the literature, or how each study builds on the work of others. In short, it does not demonstrate critical thinking.

Instead, use your outlines and notes as a guide to the important topics you need to cover, and more importantly, what *you* have to say about those topics. Literature reviews are written from the perspective of an expert on the field. After an exhaustive literature review, you should feel like you are able to make strong claims about what is true—so make them! There is no need to hide behind "I believe" or "I think." Put your voice out in front, loud and proud! But make sure you have facts and sources that back up your claims.

The term "argument" is used here in a specific way. An argument in writing means more than simply disagreeing with what someone else said. Toulman, Rieke, and Janik (1984) identify six elements of an argument:

1. Claim: the thesis statement—what you are trying to prove
2. Grounds: theoretical or empirical evidence that supports your claim
3. Warrant: your reasoning (rule or principle) connecting the claim and its grounds
4. Backing: further facts used to support or legitimize the warrant
5. Qualifier: acknowledging that the argument may not be true for all cases
6. Rebuttal: considering both sides (as cited in Burnette, 2012)

Let's walk through an example of an argument. If you were writing a literature review on a negative income tax, a policy in which people in poverty receive an unconditional cash stipend from the government each month equal to the federal poverty level, you would want to lay out the following:

1. Claim: the negative income tax is superior to other forms of anti-poverty assistance.
2. Grounds: data comparing negative income tax recipients to those in existing programs, theory supporting a negative income tax, data from evaluations of existing anti-poverty programs, etc.
3. Warrant: cash-based programs like the negative income tax are superior to existing anti-poverty programs because they allow the recipient greater self-determination over how to spend their money.
4. Backing: data demonstrating the beneficial effects of self-determination on people in poverty.
5. Qualifier: the negative income tax does not provide taxpayers and voters with enough control to make sure people in poverty are not wasting financial assistance on frivolous items.
6. Rebuttal: policy should be about empowering the oppressed, not protecting the taxpayer, and there are ways of addressing taxpayer opposition through policy design.

Like any effective argument, your literature review must have some kind of structure. For example, it might begin by describing a phenomenon in a general way along with several studies that provide some detail, then describing two or more competing theories of the phenomenon, and finally presenting a hypothesis to test one or more of the theories. Or, it might describe one phenomenon, then describe another phenomenon that seems inconsistent with the first one, then propose a theory that resolves the inconsistency, and finally present a hypothesis to test that theory. In applied research, it might describe a phenomenon or theory, then describe how that phenomenon or theory applies to some important real-world situation, and finally suggest a way to test whether it does, in fact, apply to that situation.

Another important issue is **signposting**. It may not be a term you are familiar with, but you are likely familiar with the concept. Signposting refers to the words used to identify the organization and structure of your literature review to your reader. The most basic form of signposting is using a topic sentence at the beginning of each paragraph. A topic sentence introduces the argument you plan to make in that paragraph. For example, you might start a paragraph stating, "There is strong disagreement in the literature as to whether psychedelic drugs cause psychotic disorders, or whether psychotic disorders cause people to use psychedelic drugs." Within that paragraph, your reader would likely assume you will present evidence for both arguments. The concluding sentence of your paragraph should address the topic sentence, addressing how the facts and arguments from other authors support a specific conclusion. To continue with our example, you might say, "There is likely a reciprocal effect in which both the use of psychedelic drugs worsens pre-psychotic symptoms and worsening psychosis causes use of psychedelic drugs to self-medicate or escape."

Signposting also involves using headings and subheadings. Your literature review will use APA formatting, which means you need to follow their rules for bolding, capitalization, italicization, and indentation of headings. Headings help your reader understand the structure of your literature review. They can also help if the reader gets lost and needs to re-orient themselves within the document. Assume the reader knows nothing (they don't mind) and need to be shown exactly where they are addressing each part of the literature review. It's like walking a small child around, telling them "First we'll do this, then we'll do that, and when we're done, we'll know this!"

Another way to use signposting is to open each paragraph with a sentence that links the topic of the paragraph with the one before it. Alternatively, one could end each paragraph with a sentence that links it with the next paragraph. For example, imagine we wanted to link a paragraph about barriers to accessing healthcare with one about the relationship between the patient and physician. We could use a transition sentence like this: "Even if patients overcome these barriers to accessing care, the physician-patient relationship can create new barriers to positive health outcomes." A transition sentence like this builds a connection between two distinct topics. Transition sentences are also useful within paragraphs. They tell the reader how to consider one piece of information in light of previous information. Even simple transitions like "however" or "similarly" demonstrate critical thinking and make your arguments clearer.

Many beginning researchers have difficulty with incorporating transitions into their writing. Let's look at an example. Instead of beginning a sentence or paragraph by launching into a description of a study, such as "Williams (2004) found that…," it is better to start by indicating something about why you are describing this particular study. Here are some simple examples:

- Another example of this phenomenon comes from the work of Williams (2004).
- Williams (2004) offers one explanation of this phenomenon.
- An alternative perspective has been provided by Williams (2004).

Now that we know to use signposts, the natural question is "What goes on the signposts?" First, it is extremely important to start with an outline of the main points that you want to make, organized in the order that you want to make them. The basic structure of your argument then should be apparent from the outline itself. Unfortunately, there is no formula that will work for everyone, but there are some general pointers on structuring your literature review.

The literature review generally moves from general ideas to more specific ones. You can build a review by identifying areas of consensus and areas of disagreement. You may choose to present earlier, historical studies—preferably seminal studies that are of significant importance—and close with most recent work. Another approach is to start with the most distantly related facts and literature and then report on those most closely related to your specific research question. You could also compare and contrast valid approaches, features, characteristics, theories – that is, one approach, then a second approach, followed by a third approach.

Here are some additional tips for writing the body of your literature review:

- Start broad and then narrow down to more specific information.
- When appropriate, cite two or more sources for a single point, but avoid long strings of references for a single point.
- Use quotes sparingly. Quotations for definitions are okay, but reserve quotes for when someone says something so well you couldn't possible phrase it differently. Never use quotes for statistics.
- Paraphrase when you need to relate the specific details within an article, and try to reword it in a way that is understandable to your audience.
- Include only the aspects of the study that are relevant to your literature review. Don't insert extra facts about a study just to take up space.
- Avoid first-person like language like "I" and "we" to maintain objectivity.
- Avoid informal language like contractions, idioms, and rhetorical questions.
- Note any sections of your review that lack citations and facts from literature. Your arguments need to be based in specific empirical or theoretical facts. Do not approach this like a reflective journal entry.
- Point out consistent findings and emphasize stronger studies over weaker ones.
- Point out important strengths and weaknesses of research studies, as well as contradictions and inconsistent findings.
- Implications and suggestions for further research (where there are gaps in the current literature) should be specific.

The conclusion should summarize your literature review, discuss implications, and create a space for future or further research needed in this area. Your conclusion, like the rest of your literature review, should have a point that you are trying to make. What are the important implications of your literature review? How do they inform the question you are trying to answer?

While you should consult with your professor and their syllabus for the final structure your literature review should take, here is an example of the possible structure for a literature review:

- Problem statement
  - Establish the importance of the topic
  - Number and type of people affected
  - Seriousness of the impact

- ◦ Physical, psychological, economic, social consequences of the problem
- Introduction
  - ◦ Definitions of key terms
  - ◦ Important arguments you will make
  - ◦ Overview of the organization of the rest of the review
- Body of the review
  - ◦ Topic 1
    - ▪ Supporting evidence
  - ◦ Topic 2
    - ▪ Supporting evidence
  - ◦ Topic 3
    - ▪ Supporting evidence
  - ◦ Conclusion
    - ▪ Implications
    - ▪ Specific suggestions for future research
    - ▪ How your research topic adds to the literature

Here are some additional resources, if you are having trouble putting together your literature review:

Doing a literature review

Get Lit: The Literature Review

Writing resources at the University of Texas at Arlington

The University of Texas at Arlington has several resources available to students to help with writing research proposals.

- The School of Social Work has writing resources available on its website. The Writing Guide for Social Work is available on the Writing Resources page, including the Common Assignments section and the Index of All Assignments, where students can find individual writing guides to major types of assignments.
- Check out the specific information about writing for research classes from the SSW.
- For individual tutoring assistance, the UTA Writing Center is available for in-person and live online appointments, and also has substantial walk-in office hours.

Editing your literature review

For your literature review, remember that your goal is to construct an argument for why your research question is interesting and worth addressing—not necessarily why your favorite answer to it is correct. As you start editing your literature review, make sure that it is balanced. If you want to emphasize the generally accepted understanding of a phenomenon, then of course you should discuss various studies that have demonstrated it. However, if there are other studies that have found contradictory findings, you should discuss them, too. Or, if you are proposing a new theory, then you should discuss findings that are consistent with that theory. However, if there are other findings that are inconsistent with it, again, you should discuss them too. It is acceptable to argue that the balance of the research supports the existence of a phenomenon or is consistent with a theory (and that is usually the best that researchers in social work can hope for), but it is not acceptable to ignore contradictory evidence. Besides, a large part of what makes a research question interesting is uncertainty about its answer (University of Minnesota, 2016). [1]

1. University of Minnesota Libraries Publishing. (2016). This is a derivative of *Research Methods in Psychology* by a publisher who has requested that they and the original author not receive attribution, which was originally released and is used under CC BY-NC-SA. This work, unless otherwise expressly stated, is licensed under a Creative Commons Attribution-NonCommercial-ShareAlike 4.0 International License.

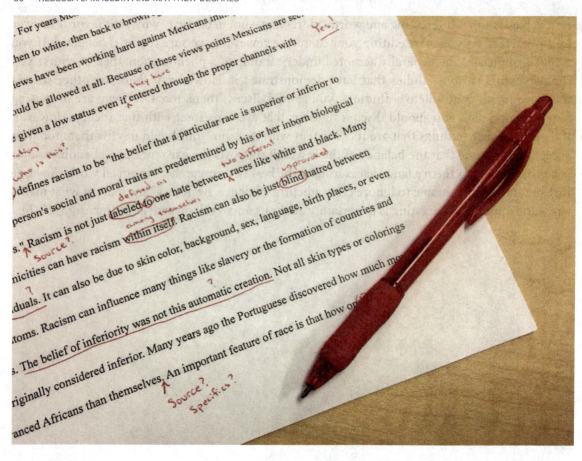

In addition to subjectivity and bias, another obstruction to getting your literature review written is writer's block. Often times, writer's block can come from confusing the creating and editing parts of the writing process. Many writers often start by simply trying to type out what they want to say, regardless of how good it is. Author Anne Lamott (1995) terms these "shitty first drafts" and we all write them. They are a natural and important part of the writing process. Even if you have a detailed outline to work from, the words are not going to fall into place perfectly the first time you start writing. You should consider turning off the editing and critiquing part of your brain for a little while and allow your thoughts to flow. Don't worry about putting the correct internal citation when you first write. Just get the information out. Only after you've reached a natural stopping point might you go back and edit your draft for grammar, APA formatting, organization, flow, and more. Separating the writing and editing process can go a long way to addressing writer's block—as can picking a topic about which you have something to say!

As you are editing, keep in mind these questions adapted from Green (2012):

- Content: Have I clearly stated the main idea or purpose of the paper and address all the issues? Is the thesis or focus clearly presented and appropriate for the reader?
- Organization: How well is it structured? Is the organization spelled out for the reader and easy to follow?
- Flow: Is there a logical flow from section to section, paragraph to paragraph, sentence to sentence? Are there transitions between and within paragraphs that link ideas together?
- Development: Have I validated the main idea with supporting material? Are supporting data sufficient? Does the conclusion match the introduction?
- Form: Are there any APA style issues, redundancy, problematic wording and terminology (always know the definition of any word you use!), flawed sentence constructions and selection, spelling, and punctuation?

Key Takeaways

- The problem statement draws the reader into your topic by highlighting how important the topic is to social work and overall society.
- Signposting is an important component of academic writing that helps your reader follow the structure of your argument and literature review.
- Transitions demonstrate critical thinking and help guide your reader through your arguments.
- Editing and writing are separate processes.

Glossary

- Signposting- words that identify the organization and structure of a literature review

CHAPTER 4: CREATING AND REFINING A RESEARCH QUESTION

Creating a research question is an iterative process, one version after another. In the preceding chapters, you started with an initial question and refined it as you learned more about the topic you're studying. In this chapter, you will finalize your research question, making sure that is it empirical, correctly structured, and feasible to answer. Once this process is completed, you'll be ready to start answering your question.

Chapter Outline

- 4.1 Ethical versus empirical questions
- 4.2 Writing a good research question
- 4.3 Quantitative research questions
- 4.4 Qualitative research questions
- 4.5 Feasibility and importance
- 4.6 Matching question and design

Content Advisory

This chapter discusses or mentions the following topics: suicide and depression, heterosexism, sexual assault, homelessness, foster care, the criminal justice system, and self-harm.

4.1 EMPIRICAL VERSUS ETHICAL QUESTIONS

Learning Objectives

- Define empirical questions and provide an example
- Define ethical questions and provide an example

When it comes to research questions, social workers are best equipped to answer **empirical** questions—those that can be answered by real experience in the real world—as opposed to **ethical** questions—questions about which people have moral opinions and that may not be answerable in reference to the real world. While social workers have explicit ethical obligations (e.g., service, social justice), research projects ask empirical questions that help support those ethical principles.

Take this example from one of Matthew DeCarlo's undergraduate research classes. A student group wanted to research the penalties for sexual assault. Their original research question was: "How can prison sentences for sexual assault be so much lower than the penalty for drug possession?" Outside of the research context, that is a darn good question! It speaks to how the War on Drugs and the patriarchy have distorted the criminal justice system towards policing of drug crimes over violent crimes. Unfortunately, it is an ethical question, not an empirical one. How could you answer that question by gathering data about people in the real world? What would an answer to that question even look like?

As the students worked on the project through the semester, they continued to focus on the topic of sexual assault in the criminal justice system. Their research question became more empirical because they read more empirical articles about their topic. One option that they considered was to evaluate intervention programs for perpetrators of sexual assault to see if they reduced the likelihood of committing sexual assault again. Another option they considered was seeing if counties or states with higher than average jail sentences for sexual assault perpetrators had lower rates of re-offense for sexual assault. These projects addressed the ethical question of punishing perpetrators of sexual violence but did so in a way that gathered and analyzed real-world information. Our job as social work researchers is to gather social facts about social work issues, not to judge or determine morality.

In order to help you better understand the difference between ethical and empirical questions, let's consider a topic about which people have moral opinions. How about SpongeBob SquarePants? In early 2005, members of the conservative Christian group Focus on the Family (2005) denounced this seemingly innocuous cartoon character as "morally offensive" because they perceived his character to be one that promotes a "pro-gay agenda." Focus on the Family supported their claim that SpongeBob is immoral by citing his appearance in a children's video designed to promote tolerance of all family forms (BBC News, 2005). They also cited SpongeBob's regular hand-holding with his male sidekick Patrick as further evidence of his immorality.

So, can we now conclude that SpongeBob SquarePants is immoral? Not so fast. While your mother or a newspaper or television reporter may provide an answer, a social science researcher cannot. Questions of morality are ethical, not empirical. Of course, this doesn't mean that social work researchers cannot study opinions about or social meanings surrounding SpongeBob SquarePants (Carter, 2010). In fact, an MA thesis (Carter, 2010) examines representations of gender and relationships in the cartoon. We study humans after all, and as you discover in your research course, we are trained to utilize a variety of scientific data-collection techniques to understand patterns of human beliefs and behaviors. Using these techniques, we could find out how many people in the United States find SpongeBob morally reprehensible, but we could never learn, empirically, whether SpongeBob is in fact morally reprehensible.

Key Takeaways

- Empirical questions are distinct from ethical questions.
- There are usually a number of ethical questions and a number of empirical questions that could be asked about any single topic.
- While social workers may study topics about which people have moral opinions, their job is to gather empirical data that guides action on behalf of clients.

Glossary

- Empirical questions- questions that can be answered by observing experiences in the real world
- Ethical questions- questions that ask about general moral opinions about a topic and cannot be answered through science

Image attributions

Spongebob by InspiredImages CC-0

4.2 WRITING A GOOD RESEARCH QUESTION

Learning Objectives

- Identify and explain the seven key features of a good research question
- Explain why it is important for social workers to be focused when creating a research question

---

Now that you've thought about what topics interest you and identified a topic that asks an empirical question about a target population, you need to form a research question about that topic. So, what makes a good research question? First, it is generally written in the form of a question. To say that your research question is "the opiate epidemic" or "animal assisted therapy" or "oppression" would not be correct. You need to frame your topic as a *question*, not a statement. A good research question is also one that is well-focused. A well-focused question helps you tune out irrelevant information and not try to answer everything about the world all at once. You could be the most eloquent writer in your class, or even in the world, but if the research question about which you are writing is unclear, your work will ultimately fall flat.

In addition to being written in the form of a question and being well-focused, a good research question is one that cannot be answered with a simple yes or no. For example, if your interest is in gender norms, you *could* ask, "Does gender affect a person's performance of household tasks?" but you will have nothing left to say once you discover your yes or no answer. Instead, why not ask, about *the relationship between* gender and household tasks. Alternatively, maybe we are interested in *how* or *to what extent* gender affects a person's contributions to housework in a marriage? By tweaking your question in this small way, you suddenly have a much more fascinating question and more to say as you attempt to answer it.

A good research question should also have more than one plausible answer. The student who studied the relationship between gender and household tasks had a specific interest in the impact of gender, but she also knew that preferences might be impacted by other factors. For example, she knew from her own experience that her more traditional and socially conservative friends were more likely to see household tasks as part of the female domain and were less likely to expect their male partners to contribute to those tasks. Thinking through the possible relationships between gender, culture, and household tasks led that student to realize that there were many plausible answers to her questions about *how* gender affects a person's contribution to household tasks. Because gender doesn't exist in a vacuum, she wisely felt that she needed to consider other characteristics that work together with gender to shape people's behaviors, likes, and dislikes. By doing this, the student considered the third feature of a good research question–she thought about the interconnections of several concepts. While she began with an interest in a single concept—household tasks—by asking herself what other concepts (such as gender or political orientation) might be related to her original interest, she was able to form a question that considered the associations *among* those concepts.

This student had one final component to consider. Social work research questions must contain a target population. Her study would be very different if she were to conduct it on older Americans or younger newly arrived immigrants. The **target population** is the group of people whose needs your study addresses. If the student noticed issues with household tasks as part of her work with first-generation immigrants, perhaps that would be her target population. Maybe she wants to address the needs of a community of older adults. Whatever the case, the target population should be chosen while keeping in mind social work's responsibility to work on behalf of marginalized and oppressed groups.

In sum, a good research question generally has the following features:

- It is written in the form of a question
- It is clearly written
- It is not a yes/no
- It has more than one plausible answer
- It considers connections among multiple variables
- It is specific and clear about the concepts it addresses
- It contains a target population

Key Takeaways

- A poorly focused research question can lead to the demise of an otherwise well-executed study.
- Research questions should address the needs of a target population.

Glossary

- Target population- group of people whose needs your study addresses

Image attributions

Question by johnhain CC-0

4.3 QUANTITATIVE RESEARCH QUESTIONS

Learning Objectives

- Describe how research questions for exploratory, descriptive, and explanatory quantitative questions differ and how to phrase them
- Identify the differences between and provide examples of strong and weak explanatory research questions

Quantitative descriptive questions

The type of research you are conducting will impact the research question that you ask. Probably the easiest questions to think of are quantitative descriptive questions. For example, "What is the average student debt load of MSW students?" is a descriptive question—and an important one. We aren't trying to build a causal relationship here. We're simply trying to describe how much debt MSW students carry. Quantitative descriptive questions like this one are helpful in social work practice as part of community scans, in which human service agencies survey the various needs of the community they serve. If the scan reveals that the community requires more services related to housing, child care, or day treatment for people with disabilities, a nonprofit office can use the community scan to create new programs that meet a defined community need.

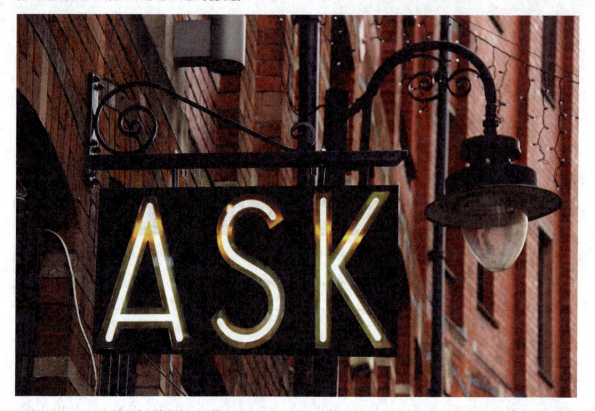

Quantitative descriptive questions will often ask for percentage, count the number of instances of a phenomenon, or determine an average. Descriptive questions may only include one variable, such as ours about debt load, or they may include multiple variables. Because these are descriptive questions, we cannot investigate causal relationships between variables. To do that, we need to use a quantitative explanatory question.

Quantitative explanatory questions

Most studies you read in the academic literature will be quantitative and explanatory. Why is that? Explanatory research tries to build something called nomothetic causal explanations.Matthew DeCarlo says "com[ing]up with a broad, sweeping explanation that is universally true for all people" is the hallmark of nomothetic causal relationships (DeCarlo, 2018, chapter 7.2, para 5). They are generalizable across space and time, so they are applicable to a wide audience. The editorial board of a journal wants to make sure their content will be useful to as many people as possible, so it's not surprising that quantitative research dominates the academic literature.

Structurally, quantitative explanatory questions must contain an independent variable and dependent variable. Questions should ask about the relation between these variables. A standard format for an explanatory quantitative research question is: "What is the relation between [independent variable] and [dependent variable] for [target population]?" You should play with the wording for your research question, revising it as you see fit. The goal is to make the research question reflect what you really want to know in your study.

Let's take a look at a few more examples of possible research questions and consider the relative strengths and weaknesses of each. Table 4.1 does just that. While reading the table, keep in mind that it only includes some of the most relevant strengths and weaknesses of each question. Certainly each question may have additional strengths and weaknesses not noted in the table.

Table 4.1 Sample research questions: Strengths and weaknesses

Sample question	Question's strengths	Question's weaknesses	Proposed alternative
What are the internal and external effects/problems associated with children witnessing domestic violence?	Written as a question	Not clearly focused	How does witnessing domestic violence impact a child's romantic relationships in adulthood?
	Considers relation among multiple concepts	Not specific and clear about the concepts it addresses	
	Contains a population		
What causes foster children who are transitioning to adulthood to become homeless, jobless, pregnant, unhealthy, etc.?	Considers relation among multiple concepts	Concepts are not specific and clear	What is the relationship between sexual orientation or gender identity and homelessness for late adolescents in foster care?
	Contains a population		
	Not written as a yes/no question		
How does income inequality predict ambivalence in the Stereo Content Model using major U.S. cities as target populations?	Written as a question	Unclear wording	How does income inequality affect ambivalence in high-density urban areas?
	Considers relation among multiple concepts	Population is unclear	
Why are mental health rates higher in white foster children then African Americans and other races?	Written as a question	Concepts are not clear	How does race impact rates of mental health diagnosis for children in foster care?
	Not written as a yes/no question	Does not contain a target population	

Making it more specific

A good research question should also be specific and clear about the concepts it addresses.

A group of students investigating gender and household tasks knows what they mean by "household tasks." You likely also have an impression of what "household tasks" means. But are your definition and the students' definition the same? A participant in their study may think that managing finances and performing home maintenance are household tasks, but the researcher may be interested in other tasks like childcare or cleaning. The only way to ensure your study stays focused and clear is to be specific about what you mean by a concept. The student in our example could pick a specific household task that was interesting to them or that the literature indicated was important—for example, childcare. Or, the student could have a broader view of household tasks, one that encompasses childcare, food preparation, financial management, home repair, and care for relatives. Any option is probably okay, as long as the researchers are clear on what they mean by "household tasks."

Table 4.2 contains some "watch words" that indicate you may need to be more specific about the concepts in your research question.

Table 4.2 Explanatory research question "watch words"

Watch words	How to get more specific
Factors, Causes, Effects, Outcomes	What causes or effects are you interested in? What causes and effects are important, based on the literature in your topic area? Try to choose one or a handful that you consider to be the most important.
Effective, Effectiveness, Useful, Efficient	Effective at doing what? Effectiveness is meaningless on its own. What outcome should the program or intervention have? Reduced symptoms of a mental health issue? Better socialization?
Etc., and so forth	Get more specific. You need to know enough about your topic to clearly address the concepts within it. Don't assume that your reader understands what you mean by "and so forth."

It can be challenging in social work research to be this specific, particularly when you are just starting out your investigation of the topic. If you've only read one or two articles on the topic, it can be hard to know what you are interested in studying. Broad questions like "What are the causes of chronic homelessness, and what can be done to prevent it?" are common at the beginning stages of a research project. However, social work research demands that you examine the literature on the topic and refine your question over time to be more specific and clear before you begin your study. Perhaps you want to study the effect of a specific anti-homelessness program that you found in the literature. Maybe there is a particular model to fighting homelessness, like Housing First or transitional housing that you want to investigate further. You may want to focus on a potential cause of homelessness such as LGBTQ discrimination that you find interesting or relevant to your practice. As you can see, the possibilities for making your question more specific are almost infinite.

Quantitative exploratory questions

In exploratory research, the researcher doesn't quite know the lay of the land yet. If someone is proposing to conduct an exploratory quantitative project, the watch words highlighted in Table 4.2 are not problematic at all. In fact, questions such as "What factors influence the removal of children in child welfare cases?" are good because they will explore a variety of factors or causes. In this question, the independent variable is less clearly written, but the dependent variable, family preservation outcomes, is quite clearly written. The inverse can also be true. If we were to ask, "What outcomes are associated with family preservation services in child welfare?", we would have a clear independent variable, family preservation services, but an unclear dependent variable, outcomes. Because we are only conducting exploratory research on a topic, we may not have an idea of what concepts may comprise our "outcomes" or "factors." Only after interacting with our participants will we be able to understand which concepts are important.

Key Takeaways

- Quantitative descriptive questions are helpful for community scans but cannot investigate causal relationships between variables.
- Quantitative explanatory questions must include an independent and dependent variable.

Image attributions

Ask by terimakasih0 CC-0

4.4 QUALITATIVE RESEARCH QUESTIONS

Qualitative research questions differ from quantitative research questions. Because qualitative research questions seek to explore or describe phenomena, not provide a neat nomothetic explanation, they are often more general and vaguely worded. They may include only one concept, though many include more than one. Instead of asking how one variable causes changes in another, we are instead trying to understand the *experiences*, *understandings*, and *meanings* that people have about the concepts in our research question.

Let's work through an example from our last section. In Table 4.1, a student asked, "What is the relationship between sexual orientation or gender identity and homelessness for late adolescents in foster care?" In this question, it is pretty clear that the student believes that adolescents in foster care who identify as LGBTQ may be at greater risk for homelessness. This is a nomothetic causal relationship—LGBTQ status causes homelessness.

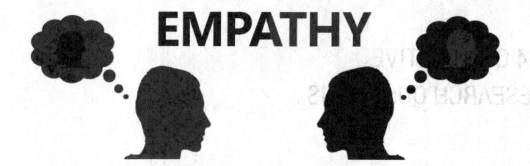

However, what if the student were less interested in *predicting* homelessness based on LGBTQ status and more interested in *understanding* the stories of foster care youth who identify as LGBTQ and may be at risk for homelessness? In that case, the researcher would be building an idiographic causal explanation. The youths whom the researcher interviews may share stories of how their foster families, caseworkers, and others treated them. They may share stories about how they thought of their own sexuality or gender identity and how it changed over time. They may have different ideas about what it means to transition out of foster care.

Because qualitative questions usually look for idiographic causal explanationsthey look different than quantitative questions. (For a detailed discussion of idiographic causal explanations, see DeCarlo (2018), Chapter 7.2). Table 4.3 below takes the final research questions from Table 4.1 and adapts them for qualitative research. The guidelines for research questions previously described in this chapter still apply, but there are some new elements to qualitative research questions that are not present in quantitative questions. First, qualitative research questions often ask about lived experience, personal experience, understanding, meaning, and stories. These keywords indicate that you will be using qualitative methods. Second, qualitative research questions may be more general and less specific. Instead of asking how one concept causes another, we are asking about how people understand or feel about a concept. They may also contain only one variable, rather than asking about relationships between multiple variables.

Table 4.3 Qualitative research questions

Quantitative Research Questions	Qualitative Research Questions
How does witnessing domestic violence impact a child's romantic relationships in adulthood?	How do people who witness domestic violence understand how it affects their current relationships?
What is the relationship between sexual orientation or gender identity and homelessness for late adolescents in foster care?	What is the experience of identifying as LGBTQ in the foster care system?
How does income inequality affect ambivalence in high-density urban areas?	What does racial ambivalence mean to residents of an urban neighborhood with high income inequality?
How does race impact rates of mental health diagnosis for children in foster care?	How do African-Americans experience seeking help for mental health concerns?

Qualitative research questions have one final feature that distinguishes them from quantitative research questions. They can change over the course of a study. Qualitative research is a reflexive process, one in which the researcher adapts her approach based on what participants say and do. The researcher must constantly evaluate whether their question is important and relevant to the participants. As the researcher gains information from participants, it is normal for the focus of the inquiry to shift.

For example, a qualitative researcher may want to study how a new truancy rule impacts youth at risk of expulsion. However, after interviewing some of the youth in her community, a researcher might find that the rule is actually irrelevant to their behavior and thoughts. Instead, her participants will direct the discussion to their frustration with the school administrators or their family's economic insecurity. This is a natural part of qualitative research, and it is normal for research questions and hypothesis to evolve based on the information gleaned from participants.

Key Takeaways

- Qualitative research questions often contain words like lived experience, personal experience, understanding, meaning, and stories.
- Qualitative research questions can change and evolve as the researcher conducts the study.

4.5 FEASIBILITY AND IMPORTANCE

Learning Objectives

- Identify the aspects of feasibility that shape a researcher's ability to conduct research
- Analyze the importance of research projects

Now that you have thought about topics that interest you and you've learned how to frame those topics as social work research questions, you have probably come up with a few potential research questions—questions to which you are dying to know the answers. However, even if you have identified the most brilliant research question ever, you are still not ready to begin conducting research. First, you'll need to think about and come up with a plan for your research design. Once you've settled on a research question, your next step is to think about the feasibility of your research question.

There are a few practical matters related to feasibility that all researchers should consider before beginning a research project. Are you interested in better understanding the day-to-day experiences of maximum security prisoners? This sounds fascinating, but unless you plan to commit a crime that lands you in a maximum security prison, gaining access to that facility could be difficult for a student project. Perhaps your interest is in the inner workings of toddler peer groups. If you're much older than four or five, however, it might be tough for you to access that sort of group. Your ideal research topic might require you to live on a chartered sailboat in the Bahamas for a few years, but unless you have unlimited funding, it will be difficult to make even that happen. The point, of course, is that while the *topics* about which social work questions can be asked may seem limitless, there are limits to which aspects of topics we can study or at least to the ways we can study them.

One of the most important questions in feasibility is whether or not you have access to the people you want to study. For example, let's say you wanted to better understand students who engaged in self-harm behaviors in middle school. That is a topic of social importance, to be sure. But if you were a principal in charge of a middle school, would you want the parents to hear in the news about students engaging in self-harm at your school? Building a working relationship with the principal and the school administration will be a complicated task, but necessary in order to gain access to the population you need to study. Social work research must often satisfy multiple stakeholders. **Stakeholders** are individuals or groups who have an interest in the outcome of the study you conduct. Your goal of answering your research question can only be realized when you account for the goals of the other stakeholders. School administrators also want to help their students struggling with self-harm, so they may support your research project. But they may also need to avoid scandal and panic, providing support to students without making the problem worse.

Assuming you can gain approval to conduct research with the population that most interests you, do you know if that population will let you in? Researchers like Barrie Thorne (1993) who study the behaviors of children, sometimes face this dilemma. In the course of her work, Professor Thorne has studied how children teach each other gender norms. She also studied how adults "gender" children, but here we'll focus on just the former aspect of her work. Thorne had to figure out how to study the interactions of elementary school children when they probably would not accept her as one of their own. They were also unlikely to be able to read and complete a written questionnaire. Since she could not join them or ask them to read and write on a written questionnaire, Thorne's solution was to watch the children. While this seems like a reasonable solution to the problem of not being able to actually enroll in elementary school herself, there is always the possibility that Thorne's observations differed from what they might have been had she been able to actually join a class. What this means is that a researcher's identity, in this case Thorne's age, might sometimes limit (or enhance) her ability to study a topic in the way that she most wishes to study it.

In addition to personal characteristics, there are also the very practical matters of time and money that shape what you are able to study or how you are able to study it. In terms of time, your personal time frame for conducting research may be the semester during which you are taking your research methods course. Perhaps, one day your employer will give you an even shorter timeline in which to conduct some research—or perhaps longer. By what time a researcher must complete her work may depend on a number of factors and will certainly shape what sort of research that person is able to conduct. Money, as always, is also relevant. For example, your ability to conduct research while living on a chartered sailboat in the Bahamas may be hindered unless you have unlimited funds or win the lottery. And if you wish to conduct survey research, you may have to think about the fact that mailing paper surveys costs not only time but money—from printing them to paying for the postage required to mail them. Interviewing people face to face may require that you offer your research participants a cup of coffee or glass of lemonade while you speak with them—and someone has to pay for the drinks.

In sum, feasibility is always a factor when deciding what, where, when, and how to conduct research. Aspects of your own identity may play a role in determining what you can and cannot investigate, as will the availability of resources such as time and money.

Importance

Another consideration before beginning a research project is whether the question is important enough. For the researcher, answering the question should be important enough to put in the effort, time, and often money required to complete a research project. As discussed in Chapter 1, you should choose a topic that is important to you, one you wouldn't mind learning about for at least a few months, if not a few years. Your time and effort are your most precious resources, particularly when you are in school. Make sure you dedicate them to topics and projects you consider important.

Your research question should also be important and relevant to the scientific literature in your topic area. Scientific relevance can be a challenging concept to assess. Here's an example. If you plan to research if cognitive behavioral therapy (CBT) is an effective treatment for depression, you are a little late to be asking that question. Hundreds of scientists have published articles demonstrating its effectiveness at treating depression. If CBT is a therapy of interest to you, perhaps you can consider applying it to a population like older adults for which there may be little evidence for CBT's effectiveness or to a social problem like mobile phone addiction for which CBT has not been tested. Your project should have something *new* to say that we don't already know. For a good reason, Google Scholar's motto at the bottom of their search page is "stand on the shoulders of giants." Social science research rests on the work of previous scholars, building off of what they found to learn more about the social world. Ensure that your question will bring our scientific understanding of your topic to new heights.

Finally, your research question should be important to the social world. Social workers conduct research on behalf of target populations. Just as clients in a clinician's office rely on social workers to help them, target populations rely on social work researchers to help them by illuminating aspects their life. Your research should matter to the people you are trying to help. By helping this client population, your study should be important to society as a whole. In Chapter 3, we discussed the problem statement, which contextualizes your study within a social problem and target population. The purpose of your study is to address this social problem and further social justice. Research projects, obviously, do not need to address all aspects of a problem or fix all of society. Just making a small stride in the right direction is more than enough to make your study of importance to the social world.

If your study requires money to complete, and almost all of them do, you will also have to make the case that your study is important enough to fund. Research grants can be as small as a few hundred or thousand dollars to multi-million dollar grants and anywhere in between. Generally speaking, scientists rarely fund their own research. Instead, they must convince governments, foundations, or others to support their research. Conducting expensive research often involves aligning your research question with what the funder identifies as important. In our previous example on CBT and older adults, you may want to seek funding from an Area Agency on Aging or the American Association of Retired Persons. However, you will need to fit your research into their funding priorities or make the case that your study is important enough on its own merits. Perhaps they are interested in reducing suicides or increasing social connectedness. These funding priorities seem like a natural fit for a study on treating depression. If you're successful, funders become important stakeholders in the research process. Researchers must take great care not to create conflicts of interest in which the funder is able to dictate the outcome of the study before it is even conducted.

Key Takeaways

- When thinking about the feasibility of their research questions, researchers should consider their own identities and characteristics along with any potential constraints related to time and money.
- Your research question should be important to you, social scientists, the target population, and funding sources.

Glossary

- Stakeholders- individuals or groups who have an interest in the outcome of the study a researcher conducts

Image attributions

Man-wearing-black-and-white-stripe-shirt-looking-at-white-printer-papers-on-the-wall by StartupStockPhotos CC-0

important by geralt CC-0

4.6 MATCHING QUESTION AND DESIGN

Learning Objectives
• Identify which research designs may be useful for answering your research question

This chapter described how to create a good quantitative and qualitative research question. In your research classes, you learn some of the basic designs that social scientists use to answer their research questions. But which design should you choose?

As with most things, it all depends on your research question. If your research question involves, for example, testing a new intervention, you will likely want to use an experimental design. On the other hand, if you want to know the lived experience of people in a public housing building, you probably want to use an interview or focus group design.

Below is a list of designs you may wish to use:

- Surveys: online, phone, mail, in-person
- Experiments: classic, pre-experiments, quasi-experiments
- Interviews: in-person or phone
- Focus groups
- Historical analysis
- Content analysis
- Secondary data analysis
- Program evaluation
- Single-subjects
- Action research

The design of your research study determines what you and your participants will do. In an experiment, for example, the researcher will introduce a stimulus or treatment to participants and measure their responses. In contrast, a content analysis may not have participants at all, and the researcher may simply read the marketing materials for a corporation or look at a politician's speeches to conduct the data analysis for the study.

As a social work researcher, you have to choose a research design that makes sense for your question and that is feasible to complete with the resources you have. All research projects require some resources to accomplish. Make sure your design is one you can carry out with the resources (time, money, staff, etc.) that you have.

Key Takeaways

- The design you choose should follow from the research question you ask.
- Research design will determine what the researchers and participants do during the project.

Image attributions

Board by geralt CC-0

APPENDICES

APPENDIX A: QUESTIONS FOR CRITIQUING QUANTITATIVE RESEARCH ARTICLES

Background	
What is the social problem being addressed? What is the research question(s) being asked?	
What has been studied or determined already? Did you identify any gaps in the current literature?	

Methods	
What is the objective of the study? Does it fall into one or more of the three categories: explanatory, evaluative, or descriptive?	
What type of research design was employed? Does the design fit the research question and social issue being addressed?	
Where and when does the study occur?	
What type of sampling was used? Was the sampling method appropriate for answering the research question(s)? Were there any potential problems with the sampling strategy that could affect the validity or generalizability of the results?	

Data	
What was most striking about the data collection and did it fit the study being conducted?	
How was data collected by the authors/researchers? Were validated instruments used to measure key variables?	

Results and Discussion	
What were the major findings of this study? Did these findings match any stated hypotheses? Were there any findings that were inconclusive or that failed to answer the research questions(s)?	
Why is this research important to the field of social work?	
What did the researchers/authors learn overall?	
What, if any, additional research is required to fully understand the issue or meet any ethical standards or guidelines?	
What are the major limitations of this study?	

Next steps	

| What stands out or is proposed for future study? | |
| What is the overall significance of the study? | |

APPENDIX B: QUESTIONS FOR CRITIQUING QUALITATIVE RESEARCH ARTICLES

Background

What is the social problem being addressed? What is the research question(s) being asked?	
What has been studied or determined already in the manuscript's literature review?	
Do you see any gaps in the literature?	

Methods

Why is this research important to the field of social work?	
What were the objective(s) and research question(s) of the study? What type of qualitative approach (e.g., narrative, grounded theory, case study, and ethnography) was used and is this appropriate to meet the objective(s) of the study?	
What sampling technique(s) was used for this study? Was it appropriate for answering the study's research questions?	
What methods were used for data collection? Who collected the data (and was this appropriate)? Was the data collected in a sufficient way for the scope of the study?	

Results and Discussion

Describe the procedures used to analyze the data. What did the researchers find during the study?	
What are the limitations of the study?	
What steps did the researchers take to ensure the rigor of the results? Specifically address trustworthiness, credibility, and authenticity. Do these steps seem sufficient?	
Are the findings adequately characterized in the manuscript's discussion/conclusions?	

Next steps

Do the authors/researchers discuss the contributions of their findings to the field of social work? Do they offer specific details of a need for further research?	
Do you agree with the way the authors interpreted their findings?	

GLOSSARY

A

Abstract– the short paragraph at the beginning of an article that summarizes its main point (2.1)

C

Comparable groups– groups that are similar across factors important for the study (4.3)

Comparison group– a group in quasi-experimental designs that receives "treatment as usual" instead of no treatment (4.1)

Compensatory rivalry – a threat to internal validity in which participants in the control group increasing their efforts to improve because they know they are not receiving the experimental treatment (4.3)

Confidence interval – a range of values in which the true value is likely to be (2.1)<

D

Diffusion of treatment – a threat to internal validity in which members of the control group learn about the experimental treatment from people in the experimental group and start implementing the intervention for themselves (4.3)

E

Empirical articles– apply theory to a behavior and reports the results of a quantitative or qualitative data analysis conducted by the author (1.2)

Empirical questions– questions that can be answered by observing experiences in the real world (4.1)

Ethical questions – questions that ask about general moral opinions about a topic and cannot be answered through science (4.1)

H

History – a threat to internal validity that occurs when something happens outside the experiment but affects its participants (4.3)

L

Literature review – a survey of factual or nonfiction books, articles, and other documents published on a particular subject (3.1)

M

Maturation – a threat to internal validity in which the change in an experiment would have happened even without any intervention because of the natural passage of time (4.3)

Mortality – a threat to internal validity caused when either the experimental or control group composition changes because of people dropping out of the study (4.3)

N

Null hypothesis – the assumption that no relationship exists between the variables in question (2.1)

P

Peer review – a formal process in which other esteemed researchers and experts ensure the work meets the standards and expectations of the professional field (1.2)

Practical articles – describe "how things are done" in practice (Wallace & Wray, 2016, p. 20) (1.2)

Primary source – published results of original research studies (1.2)

P-value – a statistical measure of the probability that there is no relationship between the variables under study (2.1)

Q

Query – search terms used in a database to find sources (1.3)

R

Reactivity – a threat to internal validity that occurs because the participants realize they are being observed (4.3)>

Resentful demoralization – a threat to internal validity that occurs when people in the control group decrease their efforts because they aren't getting the experimental treatment (4.3)

S

Secondary sources – interpret, discuss, and summarize original sources (1.2)

Seminal articles – classic works noted for their contribution to the field and high citation count (1.2)

Signposting – words that identify the organization and structure of a literature review (3.3)

Statistical significance – the likelihood that the relationships that are observed could be caused by something other than chance (2.1)

T

Table– a quick, condensed summary of the report's key findings (2.1)

Target population– a group of people whose needs your study addresses (4.2)

Tertiary sources – synthesize or distill primary and secondary sources, such as Wikipedia (1.2)

Theoretical articles – articles that discuss a theory, conceptual model, or framework for understanding a problem (1.2)

BIBLIOGRAPHY

Action Network for Social Work Education and Research (n.d.). *Advocacy*. Retrieved from: https://www.socialworkers.org/Advocacy/answer

BBC News. (2005, January 20). US right attacks SpongeBob video. Retrieved from: http://news.bbc.co.uk/2/hi/americas/4190699.stm

Bernnard, D., Bobish, G., Hecker, J., Holden, I., Hosier, A., Jacobson, T., Loney, T., & Bullis, D. (2014). Presenting: Sharing what you've learned. In Bobish, G., & Jacobson, T. (eds.) *The information literacy users guide: An open online textbook*. Retrieved from: https://milnepublishing.geneseo.edu/the-information-literacy-users-guide-an-open-online-textbook/chapter/present-sharing-what-youve-learned/

Bhattacherjee, A., (2012). Social science research: Principles, methods, and practices. *Textbooks Collection*. 3. http://scholarcommons.usf.edu/oa_textbooks/3

Blee, K. (2002). *Inside organized racism: Women and men of the hate movement*. Berkeley, CA: University of California Press;

Blee, K. (1991). *Women of the Klan: Racism and gender in the 1920s*. Berkeley, CA: University of California Press

Boote, D., & Beile, P. (2005). Scholars before researchers: On the centrality of the dissertation literature review in research preparation. *Educational Researcher 34*(6), 3-15

Burnett, D. (2012). Inscribing knowledge: Writing research in social work. In W. Green & B. L. Simon (Eds.), *The Columbia guide to social work writing* (pp. 65-82). New York, NY: Columbia University Press

Carter, A. C. (2010). *Constructing gender and relationships in "SpongeBob SquarePants": Who lives in a pineapple under the sea*. MA thesis, Department of Communication, University of South Alabama, Mobile, AL

Crutchfield, J.& *Webb, S. (2018). How colorist microaggressions have eluded social work: A literature review. *Journal of Ethnic and Cultural Diversity in Social Work*, 1-21, https://doi.org/10.1080/10665684.2015.991158

Crutchfield, J., Crutchfield, J. X., & Buford, J. (2018). Case study of school social worker as dean. *Urban Social Work, 2*(2), 106-122.

DeCarlo, M. (2018). *Scientific inquiry in social work.* Retrieved from https://open.umn.edu/opentextbooks/textbooks/scientific-inquiry-in-social-work

Early Childhood Longitudinal Program. (2011). *Example research questions.* https://nces.ed.gov/ecls/

Focus on the Family. (2005, January 26). Focus on SpongeBob. *Christianity Today*. Retrieved from http://www.christianitytoday.com/ct/2005/januaryweb-only/34.0c.html

Green, W. (2012). Writing strategies for academic papers. In W. Green & B. L. Simon (Eds.), *The Columbia guide to social work writing* (pp. 25-47). New York, NY: Columbia University Press

Green, W. & Simon, B. L. (2012). *The Columbia guide to social work writing.* New York, NY: Columbia University Press

The Guardian (n.d.). *The counted: People killed by police in the US.* Retrieved from: https://www.theguardian.com/us-news/ng-interactive/2015/jun/01/the-counted-police-killings-us-database

Hammond, C. C. & Brown, S. W. (2008, May 14). Citation searching: Searching smarter & find more. *Computers in libraries*. Retrieved from: http://www.infotoday.com/cilmag/may08/Hammond_Brown.shtml

Houser, J., (2018). *Nursing research reading, using, and creating evidence* (4th ed.). Burlington, MA: Jones & Bartlett.

Lamott, A. (1995). *Bird by bird: Some instructions on writing and life.* New York, NY: Penguin.

Leslie, M., Floyd, J., & Oermann, M. (2002). Use of MindMapper software for research domain mapping. *Computers, Informatics, Nursing,* 20(6), 229-235.

Loseke, D. (2017). *Methodological thinking: Basic principles of social research design* (2nd ed.). Los Angeles, CA: Sage

Machi, L., & McEvoy, B. (2012). The *literature review: Six steps to success (2nd ed)*. Thousand Oaks, CA: Corwin

O'Gorman, K., & MacIntosh, R. (2015). *Research methods for business & management: A guide to writing your dissertation* (2nd ed.). Oxford: Goodfellow Publishers

Ortega-Williams, A., Crutchfield, J., & Hall, J.C. (in press). The colorist historical trauma framework: Implications for culturally responsive practice with African Americans, *Journal of Social Work*

Pain, E. (2016, March 21). How to (seriously) read a scientific paper. *Science*. Retrieved from: http://www.sciencemag.org/careers/2016/03/how-seriously-read-scientific-paper

Tan, K., Teasley, M., Crutchfield, J., & Canfield, J. (2017). Bridging the Disparity Gap in School Behavioral Health. *Children & Schools*, 1-4

Thorne, B. (1993). *Gender play: Girls and boys in school*. New Brunswick, NJ: Rutgers University Press

Wallace, M., & Wray, A. (2016). *Critical reading and writing for postgraduates* (3rd ed.). Thousand Oaks, CA: Sage Publications

Webster, J., & Watson, R. (2002). Analyzing the past to prepare for the future: Writing a literature review. *MIS Quarterly*, *26*(2), xiii-xxiii. https://web.njit.edu/~egan/Writing_A_Literature_Review.pdf

Writing for Success (2015). Strategies for gathering reliable information. http://open.lib.umn.edu/writingforsuccess/chapter/11-4-strategies-for-gathering-reliable-information/

DERIVATIVE NOTES

This open textbook is based on the open textbook *Scientific Inquiry in Social Work* by Matthew DeCarlo. Licensing information can be found in the front matter. The following index details where content was used in this manuscript. New content (as noted below) indicates major additions, such as chapters, sections, subsections, or key concepts that I created.

Minor revisions not noted below include editing language for clarity, length, and flow as well as corrections to and additions of hyperlinks and citations. Other revisions not listed below include removing first person language and references to sections of the DeCarlo text that were not included in the guidebook.

Chapter 1

- Content from DeCarlo, Chapter 2
- New content in Section 1.1 contributed by Jandel Crutchfield
- Section 1.2 was reorganized with added headers and new content about Government Sources
- New content about UTA resources

Chapter 2

- Content from DeCarlo, Chapter 3

Chapter 3

- Content from DeCarlo, Chapter 4
- New content
    - Writing Resources at the University of Texas at Arlington

Chapter 4

- Content from DeCarlo, Chapter 8

Appendix A & Appendix B

- New content contributed by Brooke Troutman

LINKS BY CHAPTER

Front Matter

Mavs Open Press (https://library.uta.edu/scholcomm/mavs-open-press)

Creative Commons licenses (https://creativecommons.org/licenses/)

OER (https://library.uta.edu/scholcomm/open-education/oer)

Pressbooks Accessibility Policy (https://pressbooks.org/blog/2018/05/01/our-accessibility-policy-and-forthcoming-accessibility-improvements)

Open Education at UTA (http://libguides.uta.edu/utacares)

OER Adoption Form (https://uta.qualtrics.com/jfe/form/SV_8HTkgCym5Q6Mk7j)

BCcampus Open Education (https://open.bccampus.ca/)

Chapter 1

Dr. Jandel Crutchfield (https://mentis.uta.edu/explore/profile/jandel-crutchfield)

Encyclopedia of Social Work (http://socialwork.oxfordre.com)

Center on Budget and Policy Priorities (https://www.cbpp.org/)

SAMHSA (https://www.samhsa.gov/data/all-reports)

Drug War Rant (http://www.drugwarrant.com)

Search operators (https://tulib.tudelft.nl/searching-resources/search-operators)

CC-BY 4.0 license (https://creativecommons.org/licenses/by/4.0/)

a librarian assigned to your department (https://libraries.uta.edu/about/people/troutman-brooke)

Library Links (https://scholar.google.com/scholar_settings?hl=en#2)

databases (https://libguides.uta.edu/az.php)

inter-library loan (https://uta.illiad.oclc.org/illiad/index.htm)

Hammond and Brown (http://www.infotoday.com/cilmag/may08/Hammond_Brown.shtml)

Cochrane Collaboration (https://us.cochrane.org/)

Campbell Collaboration (https://www.campbellcollaboration.org/)

Chapter 2

The anatomy of the grid (https://www.flickr.com/photos/isriya/2189574180/in/photolist-a9Aag6-dkHnih-a9AaeP-8Zp6Uj-aPaf9T-dnWd4t-akvThj-aGy9Un-bkTacm-3GRVMW-nQvuoX-6tZCiK-s6vUhN-fmnN9M-6S5See-tokn5N-nETnGy-nEUyTv-4ku97Y)

CC BY-NC 2.0 (https://creativecommons.org/licenses/by-nc/2.0/)

gaming and narrative discussion (https://www.flickr.com/photos/bryanalexander/6737919649)

Chapter 3

Get Ready: Academic Writing, General Pitfalls and (oh yes) Getting Started! (https://ocw.tudelft.nl/wp-content/uploads/AE4010_Lecture_7a.pdf)

CC-BY 4.0 (https://creativecommons.org/licenses/by/4.0/)

example Literature Search Template (http://www.rebeccamauldin.com/resources-for-students/?preview=true)

summary table template (http://blogs.monm.edu/writingatmc/files/2013/04/Synthesis-Matrix-Template.pdf)

Literature Reviews: Using a Matrix to Organize Research (https://tcwrite.smumn.edu/wp-content/uploads/2017/10/LitRevMatrix_TC.pdf)

Literature Review: Synthesizing Multiple Sources (http://liberalarts.iupui.edu/uwc/files/documents/Lit_Review_Synthesis.pdfLiterature Review: Synthesizing Multiple Sources)

Writing a Literature Review and Using a Synthesis Matrix (https://writingcenter.fiu.edu/_assets/docs/synthesis-matrix-2.pdf)

Sample Literature Reviews Grid (https://docs.google.com/spreadsheets/d/11tXg0IYjR6kZk-Uf5Eq2pFfVSrd3lxsWOhoEqht8BZ4/edit?usp=sharing)

Literature review preparation: Creating a summary table. (https://www.youtube.com/watch?v=nX2R9FzYhT0)

Doing a literature review (https://www2.le.ac.uk/offices/ld/resources/study-guides-pdfs/dissertation-skills-pdfs/doing-a-literature-review-v1%200.pdf)

Get Lit: The Literature Review (https://www.youtube.com/watch?v=vwR82XFZdp4)

writing resources (https://www.uta.edu/ssw/student-resources/writing-resources/index.php)

writing guide for social work (http://www.uta.edu/ssw/student-resources/writing-resources/writing-guide/index.php)

Common Assignments section (http://www.uta.edu/ssw/student-resources/writing-resources/writing-guide/students/common-assignments/index.php)

Index of All Assignments (http://www.uta.edu/ssw/student-resources/writing-resources/writing-guide/students/common-assignments/index-of-assignments/index.php)

writing for research classes (https://www.uta.edu/ssw/student-resources/writing-resources/writing-guide/students/common-assignments/research-oriented.php)

UTA Writing Center (http://www.uta.edu/owl/)

Creative Commons Attribution-NonCommercial-ShareAlike 4.0 International License (https://creativecommons.org/licenses/by-nc-sa/4.0/)

Chapter 4

SpongeBob SquarePants (http://www.nick.com/spongebob-squarepants/)

Chapter 7.2 (https://scientificinquiryinsocialwork.pressbooks.com/chapter/7-2-causal-relationships)